SUPERPOWERS AND INTERNATIONAL CONFLICT

SUPERPOWERS AND INTERNATIONAL CONFLICT

Carsten Holbraad

St. Martin's Press   New York

ISBN 0–312–77674–8

Library of Congress Cataloging in Publication Data

Holbraad, Carsten.
  Superpowers and international conflict.

  Includes bibliographical references and index.
    1. World politics—1945–   2. United States—
Foreign relations—1945–   3. Russia—Foreign
relations—1945–   4. China—Foreign relations—
1949–   I. Title.
D843.H64   1979   327'.09'045   79–9942
ISBN 0–312–77674–8

Contents

Preface

In 1967–8, when I held a Canadian Institute of International Affairs senior fellowship at Carleton University in Ottawa, I began to explore the relationship between the United States and the Soviet Union. The first result was a critique of the idea of a superpower condominium or great-power concert, which many writers had advanced in the early and mid-sixties. In 'Condominium and Concert', the opening chapter of *Super Powers and World Order* (Australian National University Press, 1971), I tried to show that a high degree of joint control or collective management of international politics was an unlikely outcome of the détente in East-West relations. But important questions about the actual nature of the superpowers' diplomatic relationship and of their role in international conflict remained. Were the two giants really just 'cold monsters' in the jungle of international politics, each bent on pursuing their hostile rivalry almost regardless of the interests of everybody else, or were they also the 'great responsibles' of the society of nations, both of them anxious to restrain rivalry between themselves and restrict conflict among others, perhaps even to the point where they might attempt to engage each other in limited cooperation for the sake of maintaining a minimum degree of international order? The best way of attempting an answer, it seemed, was to examine the conduct and analyse the interaction of the Soviet Union and the United States in actual situations of serious conflict.

The transformation of the international system that followed the diplomatic rise of China and the growing independence of several other major powers gave rise to a further question. Could whatever habits of restraint or tendencies to cooperate that had developed in the dualistic system of the fifties and sixties survive and play a significant part in the more complex system that seemed to be emerging in the seventies? Dealing with that question naturally led to speculations about the possibilities of the triangle of the United States, the Soviet Union and China, and to a consideration of the patterns of conflict that might appear in a system of more than three major powers. Such was the course of the enquiry I pursued after joining the Institute of Advanced Studies of the Australian National University in 1969. This book, which was finished in 1975 and updated early in 1978, was the outcome.

I am grateful to Mr John W. Holmes of the CIIA in Toronto and to Dr R. A. MacKay, and other former colleagues, in what is now the Norman Paterson School of International Affairs at Carleton University, for their support and interest in the earlier stages of the work. It was a privilege to be able to continue my research and writing, on this and other topics, in the stimulating environment provided by the Department of International Relations of the Research School of Pacific Studies at the ANU. Among my former colleagues in Canberra, I am particularly indebted to Professors Hedley Bull, J. D. B. Miller and J. L. Richardson for critical comments on drafts of the book and useful suggestions. An earlier version of chapter 5 was presented as a paper to a meeting of the Australasian Political Studies Association in 1973, where it was subjected to trenchant and constructive criticism by Dr D. J. Ball. Chapter 6 is based on a paper read to the Strategic and Defence Studies Centre of the ANU in 1972 and subsequently published in *Cooperation and Conflict, Nordic Journal of International Politics*, No. 2 (1973). I am grateful to the editor of that journal for allowing me to use the material of my article here. Chapter 7 includes, with the kind permission of the editor of the ANU Press, an expansion of a section of my contribution to *Super Powers and World Order*. Thanks are also due to Oxford University Press and to *Soviet News* for permission to quote from documents reprinted in the collections *Documents on International Affairs*.

Athens   C. H.
May 1978

Introduction

Some memorable studies of the states system have been written in times of international upheaval, others in periods of comparative calm. Friedrich Gentz published his more trenchant treatises on the European system while Napoleon was trying to overturn this system in a bid for hegemony. Leopold von Ranke formulated his seminal ideas on the great powers and the European equilibrium in the quiet years of the restoration period. Such examples may suggest that the best writings in this field depend on a degree of correspondence between the temperament of the writer and the type of political situation in which he finds himself. A publicist gifted with passion and conviction, such as the younger Gentz, may have his deepest insights when the international system is under challenge, when he is drawn into debate about central issues and encouraged to address himself to first principles. A scholar endowed with detachment and a sense of proportion, as Ranke was, may find it easier to describe and analyse the system when a degree of order prevails, since he then can enjoy the advantage of perspective.

If perceptive studies of the states system may appear both in situations of international convulsion and in conditions of stability, the more *imaginative* writings on the subject often seem to arrive in the transition from the former to the latter type of situation, particularly from war to peace. The end of the Napoleonic Wars, as well as the conclusion of the two world wars, produced series of speculative and creative tracts on international politics. The need to replace the collapsed power structure and the opportunity to build a better international order which at the end of a major war challenge the skill of statesmen also seem to spur the imagination of writers.

In this sort of historical situation, there is a tendency to reject the principles at the root of the international structure of the recent past in favour of novel schemes for the organisation of the society of states. At the end of the First World War, for example, many Anglo-Saxon advocates of the proposed League of Nations repudiated the

I

balance of power, which they regarded as the essence of the system that had led to the war. Sometimes, however, a time earlier than the pre-war period may provide inspiration for post-war projects of international organisation. Towards the end of the Second World War some influential Western writers on international relations turned to the Concert of Europe of the nineteenth century rather than to the League of Nations in their search for a model for the Security Council of the projected United Nations.

Even the transition from cold war to détente in the relationship between the Soviet Union and the United States gave rise to a spate of visionary writings about the states system and international order. Though the relaxation of tension between the superpowers in the 1960s was less dramatic and more uncertain than that which generally occurs at the conclusion of a major war, when the great powers tend to divide into victorious allies and defeated powers, it did produce that combination of relief at having overcome an ordeal and determination to avoid similar or worse experiences in the future which seems to encourage literary attempts to reorganise the society of states. The fact that the East-West détente was accompanied by signs of a change in the international power structure in the direction of a more complex system was a further incentive to go beyond the dualistic system of the Cold War in speculating about a safer international order.

In the many books and articles about the international relations of the future that appeared in the West in the early years of détente, two ideas in particular gained prominence: that of a 'condominium' of the superpowers and that of a 'concert' of several great powers. Few of those writers who entertained the idea of a Russo-American condominium gave a precise definition of the arrangement they had in mind. But it is clear that they used the term, or its various synonyms,[1] to refer to some degree of joint control. Most of them concentrated on the control of nuclear weapons. Thus, Herman Kahn, writing early in the sixties, advocated the negotiation of a 'Hague' convention against the use of nuclear weapons:

This convention could simply set up a condominium on world affairs between the United States and the Soviet Union to the effect that they will refrain from the first military use of nucelar weapons under any circumstances and, in addition, that they will jointly constrain any third power which uses nuclear weapons in a military operation.[2]

Some described the joint functions of the partners in the condominial arrangement more generally as the management of the balance of power between the superpowers. Coral Bell, for example, suggested that the basic function of the emerging Russo-American condominium was 'joint management of the central power-balance'. If that balance could be adequately managed, the various local balances would not be likely to produce Armageddon, she thought.[3] Other writers suggested, explicitly or implicitly, that the partners might go much further than controlling the nuclear weapons of the world and managing the diplomatic relations between themselves. Arnold Toynbee, writing in an American magazine early in 1967, stated that it was:

America's and Russia's duty to come to terms with each other and to start working together, because working in partnership, they have between them, at the moment, the power to put the world in order and to keep it in order. Their present power, exercised jointly, would be irresistible. In other words, a partnership between them would be an effective form of world-government.[4]

Behind the terms 'condominium', 'partnership', etc., used by such writers, was the notion of world government by growth. Herman Kahn thought that his proposed 'Hague' convention might not only be useful in discouraging the diffusion and controlling the use of nuclear weapons but, if effective, would also be 'a major precedent for the creation of a very limited but possibly adequate "world government"'.[5] Coral Bell judged the joint resolution of the Cuban missile crisis to be more than merely an exercise in management of the central balance of power. In the superpowers' relations with Castro's Cuba she detected, also, elements of government.[6] Arnold Toynbee suggested that the benefits to be derived from the partnership he was advocating could be rather more extensive than the mere survival of the human race. Apart from making atomic war impossible, a Russo-American partnership could settle many local issues which threatened to set the world on fire, such as those of Palestine, Kashmir, Germany, Korea and China, as well as Vietnam. The partners, he thought, would even be able to make their joint power felt in domestic issues, such as those in Rhodesia and South Africa, where they could impose racial justice.[7] Yet, there is little evidence that the writers who in the sixties entertained the idea that Soviet-American cooperation could develop into informal world government had thought out the problems of setting up and maintaining an effective condominium of the world.

In their speculations about the future structure of international society, many Western writers of the last decade went beyond the declining dualistic system and envisioned a group of perhaps half a dozen great powers combining to manage international politics. In projecting a 'concert of the world', they often pointed to the model of the nineteenth-century Concert of Europe. While some suggested that the new concert might be a step towards world government, others saw it chiefly as a means of managing the balance of power.

A prominent exponent of the former way of thinking was John Strachey. If the two existing superpowers failed to establish a system of joint hegemony and to maintain their nuclear lead, he suggested in 1962, half a dozen superpowers might occupy the centre of the world stage within a decade or two. If this were to happen, it would be necessary to evolve a single centre of world nuclear authority through cooperation of all the superpowers. 'What can be envisaged for the nineteen-seventies', he wrote, holding up the old European Concert as the example, 'is "a concert of the world" in which the nuclear superpowers arrange humanity's affairs amongst themselves (and no doubt to suit themselves) and for that purpose keep the rest of the world in order, using the United Nations as their instrument.'[8] The basic agreement among the superpowers should contain at least two provisions. The first would commit the contracting parties to preventing any additional state from gaining nuclear capacity. In the second, the parties would agree to 'set upon, with all their nuclear forces, and so extinguish, anyone of themselves who, for any cause whatsoever and however just that cause might be held to be, resorted to the use of nuclear weapons'.[9] This was the old idea of collective security adapted to the nuclear world.

For Strachey, the most urgent goal was a functional world authority capable of controlling nuclear weapons, which he thought might come about through Russo-American cooperation or, failing that, by way of a wider concert of great powers. But he looked far beyond the immediate aim. Such an authority was to be 'the growth point out of which a real, political, world authority may develop'.[10] The reason he gave for aiming so high was not merely that this was the sole way to prevent nuclear war for good but also that, in the nuclear sphere, a limited functional authority was an impossibility in the long run. There was no way of circumscribing the authority of a body exercising nuclear control of the world. If the superpowers could prevent the rest of the world from acquiring nuclear arms, they could also prevent it from doing anything else.

A good example of the other view is George Liska. Writing some five years later than Strachey, he pictured a concert of the world like an instrument for maintaining the balance of power, as the Concert of Europe had been in the nineteenth century. He saw the immediate future in dualistic terms, in the shape of an informal condominium, with the United States as the leading partner. But once regions outside Europe had developed a desire and a capacity for participating in a more satisfactory international order, a reduction in the global primacy of America would be likely to follow. He projected the eventual outcome as a mixture of cooperation and competition within a group of old and new great powers. 'Such a mix of competitive-co-operative relations among greater powers is grist to the mill of a great power concert which can be no less effective for being informal and *ad hoc*.'[11] It would be compatible with, perhaps even dependent on, a distribution of regional responsibilities among the various powers. If these responsibilities came to be exercised through regional councils or organisations, the war-time idea of a regionally structured world order would come close to realisation. The United States, he hoped, would play a role in the concert of the world comparable to that of Britain in the old Concert of Europe. To be a successful concert leader, it would need 'a manifest, but unobtrusive, capacity to bring superior power to bear on the balance of power between other, more directly concerned, states'.[12] But Liska wondered whether America might not be inclined to insist on interfering unnecessarily in local issues.

A number of writers fitted both the idea of condominium and that of concert into their pictures of the future order. Strachey is one example. Though he thought that, on account of the time element, the chances of an oligarchy of super-states arising to create a single nuclear authority in a later decade were a little better than the chances of establishing a Russo-American joint nuclear hegemony in the nearer future, he did not see the two courses necessarily as alternatives. The real development of events might be a mixture of the two, with America and Russia retaining some of their nuclear predominance and four or five new nuclear superpowers forming a concert under their joint presidency.

Coral Bell, too—like Strachey, writing at the time when the bipolar balance was beginning to undergo transformation—projected a mixed system. She regarded France, or 'great-power Europe', and China as candidates for places in a multilateral balance system, as potential oligarchs. Britain, who had found a place as America's lieutenant, was already a minor member of the oligarchy. Looking to the future, she contemplated 'the potential shifts and changes in a system of four major units, with some developing elements of condominium in the position of the two greater'.[13]

Those Western writers who in the early and mid-sixties gave currency to the idea of a Soviet-American condominium in world affairs responded, on the one hand, to the need to avoid nuclear war and, on the other, to the opportunity to restructure international society which the signs of détente between the opponents of the Cold War seemed to promise. To these writers it seemed not only necessary but also just possible for the two superpowers to enter into such a relationship. In the seventies, there have not been so many advocates of condominium. In recent years the word has been used more often by opponents of any tendency towards joint superpower control of international relations, particularly by various representatives of European major powers who occasionally have found reason to fear that too close collaboration between the Soviet Union and the United States might reduce the diplomatic influence of secondary powers in Europe and elsewhere. At the present stage in time, the expectations of the earlier advocates seem rather less justified than the suspicions of the more recent opponents of Russo-American condominium. While a relationship of fairly close cooperation between the Soviet Union and the United States may be one possible outcome of the emerging triangular system of global politics, in the predominantly dualistic structure of the sixties it was hardly a likely development.

Elsewhere I have examined a number of historical cases of two dominant powers attempting to establish joint or dual hegemony in areas contiguous to them, and reached the conclusion that condominium is an unnatural relationship.[14] Rare and generally short-lived, this type of association is usually marked by tension and rivalry between the partners while it lasts. As regards the Soviet Union and the United States in the sixties, however, it may be possible to show not only that a condominial arrangement between them would have been very difficult to establish and to maintain for any length of time but also that neither party ever seriously tried to bring it about. Both the declarations and the policies of Nikita Khrushchev and John Kennedy, the chief architects of détente, and those of their successors, suggest that neither the Soviet government nor the American administration considered a superpower condominium of the world a possible or even a desirable goal.

Khrushchev's speeches contained a number of statements which Chinese and other writers of that time who were concerned about the danger of joint imposition by the superpowers were able to use in support of their charge of attempted collusion by the Soviet Union and the United States. There were, on the one hand, various broad declarations about Soviet-US cooperation for the settlement of world problems[15] and, on the other, a number of stray remarks about the superpowers shaking their fingers at any madman who might want war[16] or pulling the ears of a country which might be too war-minded.[17] But such phrases, which generally were accompanied by references to peace, international security and the destiny of the world, seem unlikely to have meant more than that Khrushchev in principle was prepared to cooperate with the Americans in preventing major war and in halting nuclear proliferation. Sometimes they may even have been inserted simply for the sake of gaining the tactical advantage of appearing to be willing to explore all possibilities of cooperation with the rival on the issue in question.

Khrushchev not only never made any explicit statement to the effect that his government was aiming at a general condominium of the world but also repeatedly denied that the Soviet leaders harboured any idea of trying to govern, manage or control international society jointly with the Americans.[18] The central idea in his détente policy was that of 'peaceful coexistence'. Believing that war was no longer 'fatally inevitable', he projected a relationship with the West which, while precluding major war, allowed keen political rivalry and economic competition. There is no evidence that Khrushchev saw such a relationship as a step towards broad cooperation and general control of the world by the superpowers, but some indication that he hoped it would create the most favourable conditions for the ultimate victory of socialism over capitalism.

In the sixties at least, the idea of superpower condominium seemed even farther from the minds of his successors than it had been from Khrushchev's. Brezhnev, Kosygin and Podgorny, as much as Malenkov and Khrushchev before them, recognised the paramount need to avoid war with the West. Through the ups and downs in Soviet relations with the United States during the Vietnam War, they adhered to the policy of peaceful coexistence. But this policy, judging by their public statements, was still aimed only at establishing what they called 'normal relations', at securing détente with the Western powers, not at bringing about an entente with the United States.

Nor is there any evidence that President Kennedy thought in terms of a superpower condominium. The idea of limited cooperation and peaceful competition, which was so conspicuous an element of Khrushchev's declared doctrine of peaceful coexistence, undoubtedly had a counterpart in Kennedy's pronouncements about East-West relations. After the dark days of Dulles's diplomacy, he introduced a note of optimism and talked a good deal about 'going beyond the Cold War'. As concerned as the Soviet leader about the danger of nuclear war, he concentrated his efforts on negotiating agreements in the field of arms control. Occasionally he also advocated limited cooperation in areas such as the scientific field. But, though he repeatedly emphasised his faith in the possibility of reaching some accommodation with the Soviet Union, a deep distrust of the intentions of the Soviet government prevented him from entertaining any notion of a more general political cooperation with the rival of the Cold War. As soon as the first euphoria after the settlement of the Cuban missile crisis had abated, he reminded Americans that Khrushchev still did not wish them well.[19] His awareness of the conflict between the long-term goal of the Soviet government and the concerns of the American nation compelled him to pay as much attention to maintaining the Western alliance as to improving relations with the East. Though the hopeful note in many of his speeches and the general direction of much of his diplomacy may have been responsible for putting the idea of Russo-American condominium into the minds of other people, in the United States and elsewhere, it is doubtful that the notion ever crossed Kennedy's own mind.

President Johnson, though he became increasingly preoccupied with the war in Indochina, continued the pursuit of détente with the Soviet Union. Like his predecessor, he stressed the common interests of the superpowers in averting world war and advocated test ban and disarmament agreements as well as cultural and scientific cooperation But the deep American involvement in the war in South East Asia and the limited Russian support of the North Vietnamese forces stood in the way of what he, too, sometimes called 'normalization' of relations between the United States and the Soviet Union.[20] During Johnson's presidency, a superpower condominium must have been regarded in official circles as something well beyond what was possible.

In the period of the Cold War, as well as in the earlier years of the détente, the Soviet and American governments undoubtedly perceived a number of important shared interests, not all of which their principal policy-makers found it wise to stress in public pronouncements. Foremost among them was the need to avert major war, which nearly all the rest of the world accepted. Also high on the list must have been a shared concern to maintain their superiority among the powers of the world, which meant restricting the build-up and the spread of nuclear weapons among secondary powers. The opposition to the nuclear test ban from Mao's China and de Gaulle's France and the lack of enthusiasm for the non-proliferation treaty displayed by these and other major countries revealed a clear conflict of interest. Furthermore, it seems likely that the two governments had recognised ever since the end of the war in 1945 that neither of them wished to see a revival of militarism in Germany, in particular, but also in Japan.[21] Finally, during the sixties they must have both come to see increasingly clearly that they had a shared interest in restraining the rise of China, whose international ambitions and stated views on how to conduct relations with the Western powers appeared then to be a growing long-term threat to peace. Yet, neither the public statements they made nor the foreign policies they pursued give one reason to think that the principal Soviet and American statesmen of the sixties ever seriously entertained the idea of a superpower condominium, in the general sense in which the term has been used here. Although, in the dualistic situation of those years, there were a number of interests and concerns which drew the two powers a little closer to each other, there were others which kept the rivals firmly apart.

In the changing situation of the early-seventies, when a global triangular system began to emerge, the nature of the relationship between the Soviet Union and the United States became more uncertain. The competition between the Soviet and the Chinese governments for closer ties with the United States, a natural result of the fear of each of finding itself faced with a hostile combination of the other two members of the triad, allowed the two superpowers to explore with greater energy than before the possibilities of establishing a more positive relationship. The progress of the first round of strategic arms limitation talks was the most spectacular sign of the new tendency to try to reach agreement and even cooperate in important spheres. It was probably indicative of the change in diplomatic relations between the two powers that President Nixon found it necessary more often than his predecessors to go out of his way to deny any intention on the part of his administration to seek to establish a Russo-American 'condominium' over the heads of European and other allies of the United States.[22]

On the other hand, the emerging triangular system itself also tends to reduce the likelihood of anything that could be described as a general condominium developing from Soviet-American attempts at collaboration. Given the continuing high level of tension between the Soviet Union and China, the United States has a clear interest in maintaining as far as it is possible an equidistant position between the two communist great-power rivals, or at least in avoiding an exclusive relationship with one against the other, which would considerably reduce its diplomatic leverage in the system. The difficulties encountered in the later rounds of strategic arms limitation talks and the recent signs of a new arms race starting between the superpowers suggest that a Russo-American condominium is a fairly remote possibility even in the triangular situation.

Though a superpower condominium of the world may have been a most unlikely outcome of the détente and may never have been the aim of either government, the idea of such an arrangement still seems a good starting-point for an enquiry into the nature of the diplomatic relationship between the Soviet Union and the United States in the later years of the dualistic system. It was, as we have seen, a key idea in the thinking of some of those Western writers who first speculated seriously about the form that the central relationship of international politics might take after the Cold War. What is more, this idea may still be behind some of the designs for superpower cooperation occasionally being advanced under the title of 'joint crisis management'. Most important of all, since condominium represents the most advanced position in a relationship between two great powers which is moving from rivalry and conflict towards agreement and cooperation, this idea makes a suitable reference point for an analysis which is aimed at determining the balance between conflict and cooperation in the actual interaction of the two superpowers.

If there are several good reasons for presenting the idea of condominium before examining the relationship of the superpowers, there is an even stronger case for relating the other key idea of the writings discussed above, that of a multiple concert, to a discussion of the more complex global system that may be taking shape in the future. Quite a few writers and other commentators are still advocating or detecting the emergence of a concert of several great powers to manage the balance of power of the world. What is more, some of President Nixon's and Dr Kissinger's projections of an 'even balance' of five great powers, which still enjoy some support among governments in various other parts of the world, may be seen as pointing in the same direction. An examination of the possibility of establishing a new concert of great powers, which takes account both of contemporary trends in international politics and of historical experience of this type of arrangement, forms a useful basis for further speculations about the various imaginable patterns of power and conflict in a global system comprising not only the United States, the Soviet Union and China but also a small number of other major powers.

The term 'superpower' has given rise to some uncertainty as to both its applicability and its definition. Nowadays 'the superpowers' is generally a collective term for the United States and the Soviet Union. But the expression was introduced well before it had become clear that these two powers were in a class by themselves. When W.T.R. Fox, as early as 1944, wrote a book about 'the superpowers', he included Britain in the category.[23] More recently, some writers have argued that China is already a superpower, while others have discussed how soon both Japan and a united Europe could become one.

The essential criterion for superpowerhood has always been might, actual together with potential. In the first post-war years Soviet might rested on the Red Army, while American might consisted mainly in possession of the atomic bomb. In later years, when both powers developed rocket weapons, the balance of forces between them found its principal expression in strategic nuclear arms. Then the essential condition for being a superpower became possession of comparable numbers of thermonuclear weapons, backed by a technological and economic potential sufficient for maintaining or increasing nuclear capability at a comparable rate. But command of large conventional military forces, backed by a huge population, was a further condition.

Lately, however, the distinction between the superpowers and those immediately below them in the international hierarchy has been blurred by the rise of a third great power. China has moved closer to the top, partly by increasing its nuclear capability to a more than significant level but mainly by entering into a triangular diplomatic relationship with the superpowers. Each of the superpowers has played a part in drawing China into interaction at the highest level, the Soviet Union by engaging in tense rivalry with this power and competing with it for a positive relationship with the United States and the United States by seeking a rapprochement with China and endeavouring to maintain some balance between the two communist rivals. Together, they have allowed the Chinese leaders to demonstrate that it is possible to assume a principal role in a global system with relatively inferior nuclear capability, without being a superpower.

The term 'superpower' was most useful at the time when the United States and the Soviet Union had only recently established themselves in a class which clearly was superior to that of those former principal powers who persisted in claiming the rank of great powers. If, as may happen, the once strictly dualistic system eventually gives way to a complex system which consists of more than three powers, it might be preferable to revive the older term 'great power' and apply it to all of the principal members of the new system, rather than to extend the meaning of the word 'superpower' to include China and Japan, and perhaps others as well.

'International conflict', the other expression in the title of this essay, describes the normal state of relations between principal powers, as well as between their allies and protégés and many other members of the states system. The term covers relationships ranging from, at one extreme, the strategic and military hostilities of all-out war to the ideological and economic rivalry of peaceful competition at the other. Usually, the course of any particular conflict is uneven, frequently oscillating irregularly between crisis and sudden confrontation, and détente and brief relaxation. While the former state always presents the danger of sliding into open hostilities, the latter sometimes gives rise to attempts at active cooperation. In the conflict with which we are concerned here, that of the Cold War and the détente years between the superpowers and their protégés, it was mainly fear of one extreme, namely war, which inspired in the sixties the idea of the two rivals overcoming their differences and moving to the opposite extreme by entering into diplomatic concert or even establishing some sort of world condominium.

This study focuses on the connection between the superpowers and international conflict. Some observers, who are impressed with the anarchical state of international life, see the superpowers as the main sources of conflict and disorder in the world—as, in the last resort, evil and dangerous monsters. Others, convinced that sovereign states form a society, regard the superpowers more as would-be regulators of conflict and pillars of order—as, at their best, responsible and effectual managers.[24] Here it will be argued that both views contain some truth, that the superpowers may be drawn towards both roles. On the one hand, the Soviet Union and the United States, locked, as they have been, in a conflict of ideology and interests, maintain the highest level of tension in the world. In their rivalry, they not only regularly use crises for their own ends but also sometimes instigate them. On the other hand, the superpowers, undoubtedly recognising certain shared interests as well as the more obvious general concerns, take trouble to control tension and friction both between themselves and between their allies and dependents. As a rule, in crisis situations, they are careful to keep conflict to sub-nuclear levels. Thus, they may be seen both as the potential wreckers and as the 'great responsibles' of the world.

The first part of this essay examines the conduct of the superpowers in actual situations of East-West conflict. Russo-American interaction in four selected crises in the international politics of the fifties and sixties is analysed with a view to ascertaining where the balance between rivalry and cooperation can be found in their relationship. The question to be answered here may be said to be whether the two powers did in fact, as has been suggested in some recent studies of international crises, develop together a number of subtle techniques for managing crises and controlling conflict or really only evolve a loose set of tacit and tentative rules for regulating conflict between themselves and their friends, in other words whether restrained rivalry remains a more correct description of their relations than limited cooperation. It is a matter of deciding how far along the road from cold war to diplomatic concert the Soviet Union and the United States travelled before the dualistic structure of international politics underwent transformation through the rise of other powers.

The second part discusses, necessarily much more speculatively, the emerging multiple system of international politics, first the simple triangle of the United States, the Soviet Union and China and then the more complex structure in which also Japan, Western Europe and India may come to play parts. The various imaginable future patterns of great-power conflict are outlined and considered, the aim here being to develop a clearer picture of the task that will confront those statesmen who in the late seventies and early eighties must exercise sufficient control on international tension to avert major war.

PART ONE
THE DUEL

'Crisis', which stems from the Greek word *krino*, decide, means turning or decision point. Though the term is employed rather loosely in a great variety of contexts, it is generally used to refer to a situation of danger or suspense. The word has gained wide currency in the language of international politics, especially in recent years, but is still without a definition generally accepted by writers in the field. For the purpose of discussing the role of third parties in crises of international politics, Oran Young tentatively defined international crisis as 'a set of rapidly unfolding events which raises the impact of destabilizing forces in the general international system or any of its subsystems substantially above "normal" (i.e. average) levels and increases the likelihood of violence occurring in the system'.[1] Coral Bell, in her study of the management of international crises, says more simply that to her mind the essence of true crisis in any given international relationship 'is that the conflicts within it rise to a level which threatens to transform the nature of the relationship'.[2] The qualities of international crisis that these definitions bring out, the imminence of violence and the threat of transformation, are those most relevant to the present study. In examining the relationship of the two superpowers in certain major crises of international politics, I shall be dealing with situations of sudden intensification of international conflict.

Writers who have done theoretical work on the subject have found it convenient to distinguish two broad categories of political and politico-military crises of international politics, namely system-wide crises and subsystem upheavals. A prominent type of the former class is the interbloc crisis, which has several varieties, including direct confrontation between leaders of blocs and clashes between lesser members. Among the subsystem crises are various types of coalition and alliance confrontations.[3] In Coral Bell's terminology, the significant difference is between adversary and intramural crises.[4] The distinctions between interbloc and intrabloc and between adversary and intramural crises, both of which apply only to a system of states divided into two or more blocs, alliances or groups, are relevant to the crises to be discussed here. But, though such distinctions are useful for analytic purposes, it is worth noting that any particular major, and in some situations even a minor, crisis is likely to present opposite aspects and, therefore, to cut across the categories. Even such an evident adversary crisis as that over Cuba in October 1962 had significant intramural implications, especially on the Soviet side, in the relationship with China. And the lesser crisis over Czechoslovakia in August 1968, though essentially an intramural upheaval, affected the East-West relationship to the extent that certain NATO forces were activated. The crises that form the subject of the following chapters present a variety of combinations of adversary and intramural elements.

In recent work on international crises, two major ways of approaching the subject may be distinguished. What might be called the intrinsic study focuses on matters such as the inner mechanisms of crisis or its several phases, perhaps with a view to determining types of crisis and depicting 'life cycles'. The extrinsic study, on the other hand, concentrates on subjects such as the causes of crisis, possibly distinguishing various levels of causation, and their effects, perhaps dealing with the questions of whether crises are only dangerous aberrations or whether they also may perform useful functions in the international political process. My work, however, falls into neither of these categories. Some of the questions raised in studies of such kinds, particularly those relating to the inner working of crises and to their effects on the conduct of the parties involved, are certainly relevant, but the concern here is with the interaction of the United States and the Soviet Union. The aim of the analysis is to find out whether, how and to what extent the superpowers acted together to influence the course of events in crucial situations of international politics. In this study, crises are means of exploring the relationship between the superpowers rather than objects of study in themselves.

The crises to be used for this purpose are those of Suez in 1956, of the Taiwan Strait in 1958, of Cuba in 1962 and of the Middle East in 1967. The period of a dozen years that they occupy stretches from the post-Stalin Cold War to the post-Khrushchev détente and spans the transition from the rigid blocs of Dulles's days to the looser alliances of Johnson's times. The four crises are well spaced in time, the concentration being on the middle and later years of Khrushchev and on the Kennedy years, the transition period in East-West relations. Moreover, they are all key crises, which exposed and tested different parts of the structure of the international system of the time. The Suez affair, though an East-West issue as well, taxed the relations between the leading Western power and its two principal allies. The clash in the Taiwan Strait, though essentially an issue between the United States and the communist bloc, had repercussions in the relationship between the leading communist power and its principal ally. The Cuban crisis, which was a direct confrontation between the superpowers, tested their relations almost to breaking-point. And the war in the Middle East, which was a clash between clients of the superpowers, again tried the central relationship of international politics. By revealing the tensions within each alliance and highlighting the conflicts between the alliance leaders, these crises mark the pattern of East-West relations in the period of the emerging détente.

Though there are real difficulties about isolating crises from the general international conflict of which they form part, and about analysing the relations of the parties in isolation from their inter-crisis relations, major East-West crises provide important material for an enquiry into the nature of the interaction of the superpowers and cast much light on the quality of their relationship. Since crises tend to make the parties more aware of the interests that divide them, major crises test the will and the ability of the powers involved to complement their competitive relationship with a degree of cooperation. The conduct of the superpowers in crisis situations shows where the balance between conflict and cooperation lies when it really matters.

In addition to the methodological difficulties hinted at above, there are problems about sources in examining superpower relations in crisis situations. Because so much less material is available from the Eastern than from the Western side, it is impossible to reach as firm conclusions about Soviet as about American policy. Nevertheless, since so much work has been done by such a variety of experts on these four crises, one is able, even when relying mainly on secondary sources and published collections of documents, to obtain a reasonably clear idea of what passed between the Soviet Union and the United States at these crucial stages of their relationship.

1 Suez 1956

In November 1956, after the British and French intervention in the clash between Israel and Egypt, the Soviet Union and the United States took certain steps to influence the course of events in the Middle East. This led many people to think that they were witnessing a revolutionary change in East-West relations. A number of European politicians who followed the developments from relatively close quarters as well as some writers who subsequently examined the diplomacy of the crisis suggested that the two powers, who had till then confronted each other in the hostility of the Cold War, had suddenly joined each other to restrain the two principal allies of the United States. Adenauer, for example, is said to have been wondering uneasily when he visited Paris on 5 November whether the United States was on the point of abandoning Europe in agreement with Russia.[1] And Mendès-France observed in the French National Assembly on 18 December that 'the political constellation was not characterised by the old opposition of three (America, France and Britain) against one (Russia), but by a new formula . . . the two biggest (America and Russia) against the two less big', which had led to the quashing of the Suez action.[2] Merry and Serge Bromberger, the French journalists who wrote one of the earliest more detailed accounts of the Suez affair, referred to 'the disconcerting agreement of the Americans and the Russians to stand behind Nasser and drive the Old World from the oil countries'.[3] And Herman Finer, who analysed the events later on from the American angle, accused Dulles of having led the United States into partnership with the Soviet Union against the best representatives of the civilisation of the West.[4] 'Was the Suez affair the first of the necessary collusions between Washington and Moscow to avoid atomic war, with the United States consequently abandoning justice for its allies?', he asked.[5] To ascertain whether the words used by these politicians and writers—'agreement', 'partnership' and 'collusion'—accurately describe the relationship of the Soviet Union and the United States over Suez, it will be convenient first to consider the actions of each of the superpowers and then to examine their interaction during the crisis.

At some stages of the crisis, the Soviet government displayed considerable diplomatic activity, putting forward motions in the Security Council of the United Nations and sending off messages to the President of the United States and the Prime Ministers of Britain, France and Israel as well as to some of the leaders of non-aligned nations. The steps most relevant to the present enquiry, however, are those which were directed at the other superpower and those which were aimed at the governments behind the Suez action, particularly the British and the French. The moves directed at the American government were mainly initiatives in the United Nations and letters to President Eisenhower. In both, the idea of joint superpower action to quash 'aggression' in the Middle East was advanced.

The debate in the Security Council on 30 October already contained hints of the line the Soviet government was going to take. After Cabot Lodge had introduced a resolution calling on Israel to withdraw its forces and on all members of the United Nations to refrain from using or threatening to use force and from assisting Israel, Sobolev presented a resolution in similar terms and made a speech in which he demanded a quashing of Israeli 'aggression'. 'May I add', the Soviet representative said, 'that the initiative of the United States in bringing this extremely serious matter so rapidly before the Security Council is warmly welcomed.'[6] In the first days of November the Soviet government, occupied with events in Hungary, took little action over the Middle East. But on the 5th Moscow initiated a diplomatic offensive. Among its various moves on that day was a note from Shepilov to the President of the Security Council requesting an immediate meeting of the Council and proposing a draft resolution, which called for cessation of hostilities towards Egypt and withdrawal of troops by Britain, France and Israel. The resolution concluded with the following passage:

> The Security Council, in conformity with Article 42 of the United Nations Charter, considers it necessary that all the United Nations member-states, and primarily the United States and the U.S.S.R., as permanent members of the Security Council which have powerful air and naval forces, render armed and other assistance to the victim of aggression, the Egyptian Republic, by dispatching naval and air forces, military units, volunteers,

instructors, *materiel* and other aid if the United Kingdom, France and Israel do not comply with this resolution in the stated time.[7]

The suggestion for joint Soviet-American military action under United Nations auspices was spelled out even more clearly in a message which Bulganin sent Eisenhower on the same day:

> . . . .The situation in Egypt calls for immediate and most decisive actions on the part of the United Nations. If such actions are not taken, the United Nations will lose its prestige in the eyes of all mankind and will collapse.
>
> The Soviet Union and the United States of America are both permanent members of the Security Council and great powers possessing all modern types of weapons, including atomic and hydrogen weapons. We bear a special responsibility for stopping the war and restoring peace and tranquillity in the area of the Near and Middle East.
>
> We are convinced that if the government of the U.S.S.R. and the United States firmly declare their determination to ensure peace, and come out against aggression, then aggression will be ended and there will be no war.
>
> Mr President, in these ominous hours when the loftiest moral principles, the foundation and aims of the United Nations are being put to the test, the Soviet government proposes to the government of the United States of America the establishment of close co-operation in order to curb aggression and end further bloodshed.
>
> The United States possesses a strong navy in the Mediterranean zone. The Soviet Union also possesses a strong navy and powerful aviation.
>
> The joint and immediate use of these means by the United States of America and the Soviet Union, on a decision of the United Nations, would be a reliable guarantee for ending aggression against the Egyptian people, against the countries of the Arab East.
>
> . . . . Such joint steps by the United States and the Soviet Union do not threaten the interests of Britain and France. The masses of the people of Britain and France do not want war, and they, like our people, want to preserve peace. Many other countries besides Britain and France are also interested in immediate pacification and restoration of the normal functioning of the Suez Canal,

which has been interrupted by the hostilities. The aggression against Egypt has not by any means been committed for the sake of freedom of navigation through the Suez Canal, which had been ensured. This predatory war was unleashed in order to restore the colonial régimes in the East that had been overthrown by the peoples. If this war is not curbed, it is fraught with the danger of, and can develop into, a third world war.

If the Soviet Union and the United States of America support the victim of aggression, other countries that are members of the United Nations will join us in our endeavours. This will greatly enhance the United Nations' prestige, and peace will be restored and strengthened.

The Soviet government is ready to enter into immediate negotiations with the government of the United States concerning the practical implementation of the aforementioned proposals, so that effective actions for peace could be taken within the next few hours.

At this grave moment in history when the fate of the whole of the Arab East and, at the same time, the fate of peace are being decided, I await your favourable reply.[8]

At 1 a.m. the following day the Soviet representative summoned the Security Council to endorse the intervention of a joint Soviet-American force in the Middle East unless the British and French forces were halted within twelve hours.

The idea of joint Soviet-American military action to defend Egypt against its arch-enemy and against the two principal allies of the United States must have been very attractive to Moscow. But it seems unlikely that the Soviet statesmen actually expected their efforts in this direction to succeed. It must have appeared almost impossible to Moscow that the American dislike of the Anglo-French venture, together with the hostile reaction of world public opinion, would be enough to make the Eisenhower–Dulles administration take steps which could bring the United States into a military clash against its strongest allies and in partnership with its Cold War adversary. However, what concerns us here is not so much the motives or expectations of the Soviet leaders as the outcome of their attempt to involve the United States in such an undertaking. What matters is that Washington, as we shall see, turned down the invitation.

The Soviet appeals to the United States were accompanied by

direct threats to Britain, France and Israel. Bulganin had already written letters to Eden and Mollet in September and October in which he stated that the Soviet Union was interested in the Middle East and could not stand aside. But it was not till 4 November that the Soviet government took strong diplomatic action. On that day, it sent identical notes to the British and French governments, protesting against the closing of certain zones in the Mediterranean and the Red Sea (this had been done in preparation for an Anglo-French invasion of Egypt) and placing the 'responsibility for all possible consequences' of this 'act of aggression' on the two governments.[9] The following day Bulganin sent the famous message to Eden in which he asserted that the Suez action was an aggressive and predatory war, carried on for colonialist reasons without any justification.

In what situation would Britain find herself [he asked] if she were attacked by stronger states, possessing all types of modern destructive weapons? And such countries could, at the present time, refrain from sending naval or air forces to the shores of Britain and use other means—for instance, rocket weapons. Were rocket weapons used against Britain and France, you would, most probably, call this a barbarous action. But how does the inhuman attack launched by the armed forces of Britain and France against a practically defenceless Egypt differ from this?

With deep anxiety over the developments in the Near and Middle East, and guided by the interests of the maintenance of universal peace, we think that the government of Britain should listen to the voice of reason and put an end to the war in Egypt. We call upon you, upon Parliament, upon the Labour Party, the trade unions, upon the whole of the British people: Put an end to the armed aggression; stop the bloodshed. The war in Egypt can spread to other countries and turn into a third world war.

The Soviet government has already addressed the United Nations and the President of the United States of America with the proposal to resort, jointly with other United Nations member-states, to the use of naval and air forces in order to end the war in Egypt and to curb aggression. We are fully determined to crush the aggressors by the use of force and to restore peace in the East.

We hope that at this critical moment you will show due common sense and draw the appropriate conclusions.[10]

On the same day Bulganin sent a similar letter to Mollet, in which he made the same points, and one to Ben-Gurion, in which he said that he was recalling the Soviet Ambassador from Tel Aviv. Moscow Radio broadcast the contents of these communications before they reached those to whom they were addressed, adding threats of force rather more direct than those implied in the written messages. Soon after, Moscow Radio began carrying appeals for volunteers for Egypt. On the 10th, the Tass News Agency released a statement in Moscow which pointed out that it had been stated in leading Soviet circles that if Britain, France and Israel, contrary to the decisions of the United Nations, did not withdraw all their troops from Egyptian territory and remove the threat of renewal of military operations against Egypt, 'then the appropriate authorities of the U.S.S.R. will not hinder the departure of the Soviet citizen volunteers who wish to take part in the struggle of the Egyptian people for their independence'.[11] The threat to send volunteers was repeated during the following week and was not removed till 8 December, when the British, French and Israeli forces had been instructed by their governments to withdraw.

In the years after the crisis there was a good deal of debate about the nature of the Soviet menaces and their effects on the three governments behind the Suez action. Some writers attached little importance to the threats. Hans Speier, for example, pointed out that, despite the menacing form and the rude language of the messages of 5 November to Eden and Mollet, the threat of using rockets against Britain and France fell short of explicitly mentioning atomic and hydrogen weapons and was couched in the non-committal form of a conditional question. It was far from being an ultimatum. Furthermore, the severity of the notes was reduced by Bulganin's message to Eisenhower and by Shepilov's letter to the President of the Security Council. It was clear, Speier concluded, that what the Soviets were thinking of was military intervention in Egypt rather than rocket warfare against Britain and France, in other words that the lesser threat of sending volunteers and arms was the real one.[12] Walter Z. Laqueur even questioned whether Moscow was really willing to send volunteers to fight in Egypt, and thus risk a world war. Soviet timing, he argued, suggested that the threats were made only after it must have seemed virtually certain to Moscow that it would not be necessary to follow them up with action. While the letters to Eden, Mollet and Ben-Gurion were not sent until it had become clear that the United States would not intervene, the official statement about sending volunteers was not issued until the armistice in Egypt had already come into force.[13]

The Brombergers reported that Mollet and Eden, who held a telephone conversation after receiving Bulganin's messages, agreed that the Soviet talk of atomic missiles was a bluff designed to impress the Arab countries and make them think that the Soviet Union was the defender of Egypt.[14] Eden confirms in his memoirs that the British government 'considered that the threats in Marshall Bulganin's note need not be taken literally'.[15] And when French Foreign Minister Pineau, on 19 December 1956, listed the four factors that had made the allies decide to stop the hostilities, he put Russian intervention last.[16] Even Nasser, looking at the issue from a rather different angle, made the same point when he said that the Russians had been of limited use.[17]

A number of writers, however, have argued that the Russian threats were more important at the time than some of the people involved in the crisis cared to admit afterwards. M. S. Venkata-ramani, for example, has pointed out that there were many who believed that it was the Soviet threat of missile warfare rather than the United Nations resolutions and the American pressures which forced Britain and France to withdraw their troops.[18] O. M. Smolansky has suggested that it might be hindsight which made Eden, Mollet and Ben-Gurion maintain that they had attached least importance to the Russian intervention. In support of the view that there was some alarm at the time, Smolansky refers to the memoirs of Robert Murphy, who was in London during part of the crisis and who reported that Eden was more affected by Bulganin's message than he liked to show.[19]

But whatever importance the Soviet moves may have had in comparison with other factors influencing the decision-making of the British and French governments at the height of the crisis, few writers have denied that these threats had *some* influence on the course of events. The fact that the Soviet leader referred, albeit conditionally to the possibility of missile warfare was enough for his messages to receive serious attention. The American government could no more afford to ignore a threat of this nature directed at its allies than could the allied governments themselves. And the explicit threat of sending volunteers to help Egypt, which, though less ominous, seemed rather more plausible, was bound to be relevant to the government's considering how to proceed with the invasion. For the purpose of this inquiry it is enough to note that the

Soviet pressure was of some significance to the parties involved in the Suez action. The question that concerns us is not whether the Russian diplomatic intervention was more or less effective than the American, but whether the superpowers in any way coordinated their efforts to restrain the other powers and control the course of the crisis. To answer this question, it is necessary to look at the conduct of the United States in the crisis and to examine its response to the appeals from the Soviet Union as well as its reactions to the initiatives of its allies.

The message from Bulganin made a strong impression when it reached Washington in the afternoon of 5 November. According to Herman Finer, whose account, it must be borne in mind, is extremely critical of the US administration's handling of the crisis, the President and his advisers became terrified. They feared that the Soviet leaders, afraid that the Western powers would support the rebellions in Eastern Europe, might take advantage of the division between the United States and its principal allies to embark on major aggression. The President, Finer reports, even regarded Bulganin's letter as a kind of ultimatum, which might precede an attack. Those in the administration as well as some people on the Policy Planning Committee, he states, were so terrified of nuclear war that they actually talked about the world being 'fried to a crisp'.[20] Hugh Thomas, too, says that there was semi-panic in Washington after the receipt of Bulganin's message.[21] Robert Murphy, however, though agreeing that some people in Washington were alarmed, maintains that the President himself was unperturbed.[22] The reactions of the American government to this situation took two directions, one towards the Soviet Union, the other towards the three allies of the Suez action.

An answer to Bulganin's message was drawn up with unusual speed. Within hours of the receipt of the letter the White House released the following statement on the President's reply:

The President has just received a letter from Chairman Bulganin which had been previously released to the press in Moscow. This letter – in an obvious attempt to divert world attention from the Hungarian tragedy—makes the unthinkable suggestion that the United States join with the Soviet Union in a bipartite employment of their military forces to stop the fighting in Egypt.

The Middle East question—in which there has been much

provocation on all sides—is now before the United Nations. That world body has called for a cease-fire, a withdrawal of foreign armed forces, and the entry of a United Nations force to stabilize the situation pending a settlement. In this connection, it is to be regretted that the Soviet Union did not vote last night in favor of the organization of the United Nations force. All parties concerned, however, should accept these United Nations resolutions promptly and in good faith.

Neither Soviet nor any other military forces should now enter the Middle East area except under United Nations mandate. Any such action would be directly contrary to the present resolution of the United Nations, which has called for the withdrawal of those foreign forces which are now in Egypt. The introdution of new forces under these circumstances would violate the United Nations Charter, and it would be the duty of all United Nations members, including the United States, to oppose any such effort.

While we are vitally concerned with the situation in Egypt, we are equally concerned with the situation in Hungary. There, Soviet forces are at this very moment brutally repressing the human rights of the Hungarian people. Only last night the General Assembly in emergency session adopted a resolution calling on the Soviet Union to cease immediately its military operations against the Hungarian people and to withdraw its forces from that country. The Soviet Union voted against this resolution, just as it had vetoed an earlier resolution in the Security Council. The Soviet Union, is, therefore, at this moment in defiance of a decision of the United Nations, taken to secure peace and justice in the world.

Under these circumstances, it is clear that the first and most important step that should be taken to insure world peace and security is for the Soviet Union to observe the United Nations resolution to cease its military repression of the Hungarian people and withdraw its troops. Only then would it be seemly for the Soviet Union to suggest further steps that can be taken toward world peace.

Since Chairman Bulganin has already released his letter to the President, it is proper now to release a letter written by the President yesterday to the Chairman about the situation in Hungary.[23]

Describing as unthinkable the suggestion of a joint employment of military force to stop the fighting in Egypt amounted to a complete rejection of the Soviet appeal for cooperation. The declaration of an intention to oppose any unilateral Soviet action in the Middle East was a further rebuff; and the strong language about the Soviet government's handling of the Hungarian crisis was a return of attack. The total effect of the statement was to underline the sharp opposition between the two blocs.

The references in Bulganin's messages sent to the three Western statesmen to rocket weapons, atomic and hydrogen arms and a third world war, which could be seen as an implied threat of all-out war, were not taken up in this statement. But it is known that Eisenhower made it clear to the Soviet leaders that the United States intended to retaliate in the event of a nuclear attack on Britain and France. Backing his words with action, the President ordered an alert of the air defence command and the dispatch of aircraft carriers into European waters.[24] NATO, too, was alerted. On 13 November General Gruenther, Commander in Chief of the NATO forces in Europe, defined the position in the clearest terms. 'If the Soviet Union carried out its threat to use guided missiles against Western European countries,' he explained, 'we should immediately retaliate and the Soviet Union would be destroyed. That is as certain as that night follows day.'[25] When the American administration decided to interpret Bulganin's references as a threat and to respond with a warning of nuclear retaliation, and to back the warning with precautionary military measures, the crisis in the relations between the superpowers assumed some of the character of confrontation.

The American government brought influence to bear on the allies of the Suez action both through the United Nations and through direct contacts. In the earlier phase of the crisis, up till 5 November, the United Nations seemed to be the principal venue. But immediately after receipt of the letter from Bulganin as well as in the later stages of the crisis, direct pressure in the capitals of the allies, especially London, became the more important course of action. When news of the Israeli attack reached Washington on 29 October, Dulles announced that he would refer the matter to the Security Council. On the following day Cabot Lodge introduced the draft resolution already mentioned, which called on Israel to withdraw its forces and on all members of the United Nations to refrain from using force and to withhold all assistance from Israel. This resolution—which followed direct recommendations and warnings from Eisenhower to Ben-Gurion delivered the previous days—was vetoed by Britain and France, as was the similar draft resolution presented by the Soviet Union.

As soon as it became known that Britain and France had delivered an ultimatum to Egypt and Israel, Eisenhower appealed to the Prime Ministers in London and Paris to refrain from following up with intervention. After the ultimatum had expired and Egypt had been bombed, Dulles, angry that he had been left in the dark about the plans of his allies, expressed his 'extreme displeasure' to the British Chargé d'Affaires.[26] The next step, however, was taken at the United Nations again. When the Security Council had been halted by the British and French veto, the General Assembly was brought into action. On 1 November it met in emergency session and, despite British and French objections, considered a draft resolution introduced by Dulles. This resolution, which was passed with a very large majority, urged 'that all parties now involved in hostilities in the area agree to an immediate ceasefire and, as part thereof, halt the movement of military forces and arms into the area'. It further urged that the parties to the armistice agreements withdraw all forces behind the armistice lines, and decided that the General Assembly should remain in emergency session until the resolution had been complied with.[27]

After the exchange with Bulganin a new urgency descended in Washington. Having decided to rebuff the Soviet leaders and turn down their appeal for joint action, Eisenhower and his advisers found it imperative to check the allies immediately and put a stop to the Suez action. By telephone as well as through normal diplomatic channels the President put strong pressure on the governments concerned, especially the British. In accordance with the stance taken by the Americans in response to the Soviet diplomatic move, the two European allies were assured that the Atlantic Alliance held good and that the atomic 'umbrella' still covered Western Europe.[28] But at the same time it was made clear to London and Paris that Washington could not be relied on to assist the 'aggressors' if they found themselves confronted with units of Soviet volunteers in the Middle East.[29] In effect, the British and French governments were told that, while they were protected against the larger Soviet threat, they were on their own if Moscow decided to carry out its lesser, but much more credible, threat.

Having indicated to its allies how it would be likely to react to any military move by the other superpower, the American government took further measures to eliminate the situation that might give rise to Soviet intervention. It demanded a cease-fire, backing the demand with warnings and various forms of pressure. On the night of 5/6 November Eisenhower telephoned Eden and, according to accounts, told him rudely, 'I demand that you immediately give the cease-fire order, if you want to preserve Anglo-American solidarity as well as peace. I cannot wait any longer.'[30] The order was to take effect by midnight on the 6th. Similar pressure was applied in Paris, where ambassador Dillon delivered a note to Mollet on 6 November. 'If you continue with your culpable attitude do not count on us' was the message of this warning. Eisenhower himself is said to have told the French ambassador in Washington that he was at the end of his tether and that he would stick to the UN Charter to the end.[31] Ben-Gurion, too, received a message that if Russia attacked his country he would receive no assistance from the United States.[32] Apparently to bring home its pressure on Britain, the United States government seemed deliberately slow in coming to the rescue of its ally when an alarming flight from the pound developed, agreeing eventually to approve a loan only on the condition that the cease-fire was ordered as demanded.[33]

After the cease-fire, the Americans maintained the pressure on the British and French governments in order to secure compliance with the United Nations resolutions. While they, officially at least, curtailed oil supplies to the European market, they also withheld dollar credits when they were needed.[34] In addition to economic sanctions or threats of this nature, the American government took the step of cancelling Eden's visit to the United States, making it a condition for a later meeting between him and Eisenhower that Anglo-French forces were withdrawn from Egypt. In his memoirs, Eden complains that the United States government hardened against its ally on almost every point and actually became harsher after the cease-fire than it had been before.[35]

If the effect of the Soviet messages on the British and French governments is debatable, there is little doubt that the pressure from America was an important influence on decision-making in London and Paris after the crisis reached its height. The British government was particularly susceptible to American influence, especially after the run on the pound had started. Following Eisenhower's call to London, Eden took the decisive step of telephoning Mollet in Paris to call off the action in Suez. He was cornered and left alone, the Prime Minister said. Insisting that it was impossible for Britain to go it alone without the United States, he refused to give way to Mollet's pleadings to continue the action.[36] Of course, there were factors other than diplomatic pressure and economic threats from Washington to influence Eden in the critical hours of the crisis, among them the division of public, parliamentary and cabinet opinion in Britain and the almost universal condemnation of world opinion. But ultimately it was the need to maintain the relationship with the United States which forced the British to give way.

The four major powers involved in this crisis interacted through a series of pressures on each other: the Soviet Union on Britain and France and on the United States; the United States on the Soviet Union and on Britain and France; and Britain on France. The Soviet pressure on the United States was largely indirect, mainly taking the form of threats to its principal allies. The American pressure on the Soviet Union, however, was direct, which gave the crisis an element of confrontation. While the pressure of the Soviet Union on Britain and France was exerted through military threats and carried out in the open, that of the United States on the same powers was employed through economic and diplomatic influence and was applied secretly.

The manner in which the Americans brought their influence to bear on the British and the French was a significant feature of this set of interlocking pressures. Even at the height of the crisis, Eisenhower and Dulles were careful to avoid unnecessary affront to the governments of the two allies. In his radio and television broadcast of 31 October, Eisenhower went no further in condemning the Anglo-French action than saying he believed it 'to have been taken in error'. At the same time he made a point of emphasising the friendship with the two countries, declaring his determination to retain and strengthen the bonds with them.[37] Later on the exact nature of the sanctions applied or threatened by the American government after 5 November was for long kept secret from the public. Throughout the crisis, it seems clear, the United States generally conducted relations with its two allies with an eye to maintaining the Western position in the rivalry with the Eastern bloc. Thus, not only the British but also the Americans subordinated the intramural issue, the essence of the crisis, to the adversary conflict.

The actions taken by the superpowers to deal with the crisis could be best described as parallel. While their initiatives in the United

Nations after the Israeli aggression followed similar lines, the influence they brought to bear in the capitals of Britain, France and Israel in the days before 6 November as well as the following weeks had identical aims, namely to stop the Suez action and secure a withdrawal of the forces of the intervening powers. But there is no evidence to suggest that the superpowers concerted their efforts, or even that they both ever seriously considered the possibility of cooperating in the settlement of the crisis. When one superpower called for joint action, the other answered that the idea was unthinkable. Each then proceeded independently. Even to say that 'effective, though tacit, Soviet-American coordination' character-ised the Suez crisis would be to go too far.[38] Neither party, it seems, was intent on bringing its own efforts into harmony with those of the other.

The Soviet Union and the United States moved along parallel lines largely because they were motivated by similar, and compet-ing, interests. For strategic and economic reasons, each wanted to strengthen its position in the Middle East and remain on good terms with the oil countries. The Soviet Union, probably keen to gain physical presence in the region without offending Arab opinion, threatened to intervene with 'volunteer' forces. The United States, anxious to prevent its rival from increasing its influence in a region which had been hitherto regarded as a Western sphere of interest, put pressure on the 'aggressors' to end the hostilities before they could lead to a wider war. Similarly, both powers found it in their interest not to offend world public opinion, especially its Afro-Asian section, by condoning what was widely regarded as a 'colonialist' act of intervention. So, while the Soviet Union posed as the would-be defender of Arab interests against imperialist plotters, the United States thwarted the designs of Egypt's enemies.

Parallel but separate moves, however, describe only one side of Russo-American interaction in that crisis. The other side was active rivalry, stemming from the conflict of interests in the Middle East and elsewhere, the clash of ideologies and the Cold War tradition of hostility between the two camps. At the height of the crisis, when the Soviet government put pressure on the United States by threatening its allies and the American government responded with a verbal warning and an alerting of its forces, the superpowers were on the threshold of confrontation. The events in Hungary further exacer-bated the antagonism. If the Soviet government may be suspected of having built up East-West tension over the Middle East partly at least to divert attention from its actions in Hungary, Dulles's strong reaction to the Anglo-French intervention may be explained partly in terms of his frustration at seeing an opportunity to denounce the Soviet government before the world being impaired by events in the Middle East.

Both parties, however, exercised considerable restraint in the tense situation that developed after 5 November. The Soviet Union avoided putting direct pressure on the opponent and even hedged its threats to Britain and France by appealing to the United States for cooperation. The United States balanced measured pressure on the opponent with a strong demand of its allies to eliminate the situation that might invite Soviet intervention. If the Russians exercised caution mainly out of awareness of America's preponderance of power, the Americans probably acted with care partly at least from fear of a wider and much more dangerous war. As conflicts of interest and ideology prevented the superpowers from cooperating in the termination of the crisis, so mutual fear of a major East-West clash stopped them from engaging in all-out rivalry.

Far from being a case of 'cooperation' or 'collusion', the interaction of the superpowers in the Suez crisis, it may be concluded, was a mixture of parallel action towards third parties and restrained rivalry between themselves. The separate efforts of the two powers to check the allies of the Suez action stemmed largely from competing interests. As an essay in joint crisis management, the handling of this crisis was not impressive.

An important effect of the Suez crisis was to reduce the influence of Britain and France in the Middle East and their standing in world politics. Before the events of 1956 Britain and France, who had been principals at the Geneva Conference of 1954, could still regard themselves as world powers. After their withdrawal from Suez it was much more difficult for both them and others to do so. If their intervention in the clash between Israel and Egypt could be seen, from one point of view, as an attempt to demonstrate their ability to pursue policies independently not only of their superpower adversary but also of their superpower ally, in other words as a challenge to both of the superpowers, the reactions of the United States and the Soviet Union to the Anglo-French initiative might be seen as responses to such a challenge. By decisively thwarting these attempts to act as great powers, the superpowers pushed the two European powers into secondary positions in a region in which, despite various failures in the past, they had been the major external powers till quite recently. Thus Britain and France were reduced to the rank of middle powers in both Middle Eastern and Global politics.

But, though the crisis demonstrated that the global superiority of the superpowers extended to a region in which Britain and France were particularly interested, it did not lead to a split between the two European powers and their superpower ally. On the contrary, the pressure exerted by the superpowers forced especially Britain but also France into the hands of the United States. Despite the tension that arose between the alliance leader and its two principal allies and despite the later development in relations with France, the immediate effect was a strengthening of the leadership of the United States. Unlike the next two crises to be examined here, which had much more serious repercussions for the relationship between one of the superpowers and its principal ally, the Suez crisis left the two blocs intact – extending the contact and rivalry between them to a region which was to prove fruitful for other East-West clashes.

2 Taiwan Strait 1958

The rather complex structure of the crisis over the offshore islands in the Taiwan Strait in 1958 makes it a little more difficult to analyse than some East-West crises. Three patterns of conflict may be distinguished in this confrontation. On one level was the clash between the Chinese People's Republic and Nationalist China. This local, bilateral issue could be seen as part of an unfinished civil war, an interpretation which both the CPR and the Soviet Union found it convenient to uphold in the later stages of the crisis. On another level was the wider conflict between the Soviet Union and the CPR on one side and Nationalist China and the United States on the other. Here the crisis had intramural as well as adversary aspects. Superimposed on these patterns was the triangular conflict involving the two Chinas and the United States. As the crisis developed, this particular pattern of interaction became the dominant one. However, since our concern is with the conduct of the two superpowers, especially with their willingness and ability to manage international crises, it is necessary to concentrate on the roles of the Soviet Union and the United States and to pay far less attention to the parts played by their allies in the Far East. It is convenient to discuss first the relations of the Soviet Union with the CPR and then the relations of the United States with Nationalist China and finally, after a brief look at the relationship between the United States and the CPR, to examine the interaction between the two superpowers in the crisis.

The Sino-Soviet debate some years later over the part played by the Soviet Union in this crisis has a faint echo in the writings of Western scholars. Most writers on the subject have tended to accept the Chinese accusation that Soviet support for the venture against Taiwan was inadequate and untimely. Thus, John R. Thomas, writing a few years after the crisis, found that all the evidence suggested that extreme caution had governed Soviet conduct throughout the crisis.[1] When the danger of conflict had been greatest, namely in the military phase between 23 August (when the

Communist Chinese started shelling Quemoy) and 6 September (when the CPR offered to resume negotiations with the United States), the Soviets had spoken softly. During this period, the Soviet government had seemed more concerned to avoid exacerbating the conflict to the point of general war than to support its ally in a conflict with the enemy. Only after the crisis had moved into a political phase, Thomas pointed out, had the Soviets resorted to some menacing threats. Since by then there had been little danger of war between the superpowers, his argument ran, the Soviets' threats had been made essentially for political effect. At best, their purpose had been to cover a retreat by the CPR, not to advance its aims. Altogether, the behaviour of the Soviet Union had played a large part in the humiliation of its ally.

Donald S. Zagoria, writing about the same time, agreed with Thomas that the apparent issue between the Soviet Union and China during the crisis had reflected a general disagreement on global strategy.[2] This disagreement, which had emerged also in the debate about how to react to affairs in the Middle East in the preceding months, had been about the way of responding to the United States. While the Chinese seemed to have been of the opinion that brinkmanship by the imperialists must be answered in kind, the Russians had apparently taken a more cautious view. At Khrushchev's meeting with Mao in Peking at the end of July, the latter had presumably argued the case for initiating a bitter struggle in the Taiwan Strait, but he seemed to have been unsuccessful in convincing the Soviet leader. Otherwise their joint communiqué of 3 August would probably have made some mention of the Taiwan 'liberation' theme, which had occupied a central place in the Chinese propaganda of the time. For his policy of interdiction of the offshore islands, Zagoria thought, Mao had needed an early, firm, public and high-level Soviet commitment of at least moral support for 'liberation'. That Khrushchev subsequently, in the earlier stages, had de-emphasised the crisis was perhaps a sign that he had found the venture too risky. It was even possible that Moscow had refused to give Peking a definite assurance of tactical nuclear support unless the Chinese first took some of the pressure off the offshore islands and reduced the risk of an extension of conflict. At any rate, strong Soviet expression of support for Peking had come only after Chou En-lai had offered to negotiate. Even then Khrushchev had sought to steer a middle course by pledging himself to aid China immediately if it were attacked by the Unites States but avoiding committing himself to help China evict American forces from the Taiwan Straits. Looking back at the crisis and judging from the secret documents exchanged by the two parties in 1960, Zagoria found good reason to believe that the Russians had seriously feared that they might be dragged into a general war, whilst the Chinese had resented receiving inadequate support from their ally.

Alice Langley Hsieh, too, suggested that the difference between the Soviet Union and Communist China on their estimations of the global balance of forces and their interpretations of the strategic situation had led them to disagree seriously about the action in the Taiwan Strait.[3] Like Zagoria, she thought that one purpose of Khrushchev's sudden visit to Peking had been to discourage the Chinese from launching operations in the Far East which could lead to general war. While Peking no doubt had hoped for a Soviet commitment, the Russians had held back in order to avoid getting involved in a war with the United States. Harold C. Hinton, writing four years later, generally followed this interpretation, noting Moscow's obvious lack of enthusiasm at the outset, its restraining influence and limited support in the earlier phase, and its 'pained neutrality' in the later stage of the crisis.[4]

But some writers have challenged such interpretations of the evidence and have argued that the Soviet Union and China may have had no major disagreement about strategy during the crisis. Thus, Morton H. Halperin and Tang Tsou, in a joint study published in 1967, suggested that the Soviet government did not object to the Chinese probe in the Taiwan Strait, that the Chinese government did not seek a larger Soviet role, and that neither country emerged from the crisis feeling that the other had let it down.[5] At the Peking meeting, in the opinion of these authors, the two leaders had very likely agreed on general strategy as well as on the role of each power in the projected venture. Perhaps Khrushchev had liked the idea of letting the Chinese take the sort of action in the Far East that they themselves had demanded from the Soviets in the Middle East, in which case he had probably promised Mao the support that the Chinese had requested.

Throughout the crisis, it seemed to Halperin and Tsou, Mao had received exactly the support he might have been promised. In the earlier stages, when the Chinese apparently had hoped to capture the offshore islands without American intervention, Mao had probably wanted only very general and low-level statements of support from his ally. This form of support would not only have

seemed more likely to keep the United States out of the crisis but
would also have allowed China to deal with its 'civil war' on its own,
without *any* of the superpowers interfering. It was in the later stages
of the crisis, after 6 September, when an American attack on the
Chinese mainland appeared to have become a distinct possibility,
that Mao had needed a strong, high-level statement of support from
his ally, Halperin and Tsou argued. Unlike the other writers
discussed here, who tended to distinguish between an earlier,
military and a later, political and much less risky phase, these
authors maintained that there had been no serious risk of a nuclear
clash with the United States in the earlier stage. This danger, they
suggested, had arisen only after Dulles's statement committing the
United States to the defence of Quemoy and announcing the plan
for escorting Chinese Nationalist supply vessels and after the
subsequent change in Chinese tactics on 6 September, when Chou
En-lai called for a reopening of Sino-American ambassadorial talks.
By implication, Chou En-lai's move had acknowledged America's
direct involvement in the crisis. The fact that Khrushchev had sent
his strong letter of warning to Eisenhower at the outset of this more
dangerous phase of the crisis, namely on 7 September, indicated
clearly, the argument continued, that the Soviet government had
been confident that the Chinese could be relied on to exercise
enough restraint to avoid a direct military clash with the United
States, which could have led the Soviet Union into a nuclear war
with its fellow superpower.

Halperin and Tsou were also inclined to think that there had
been nothing in Khrushchev's later clarifications of his commitment
which the Chinese could have found either objectionable or
unsatisfactory. His anwer to a TASS correspondent on 5 October,
when he reiterated the Chinese claim that their attempt to liberate
the offshore islands and Taiwan was a purely internal affair and
asserted that any attack on China by the United States would
involve the Soviet Union, might even have been given at the request
of the Chinese government, they thought. The conclusion of their
argument was that neither the behaviour of Russia nor that of
China in the crisis could have caused a serious quarrel and led to a
split between them. The two authors supported this finding with a
study of the Sino-Soviet polemics of 1963, which indicated that
disagreement between the two powers had reached serious proportions only some time after the end of the crisis in the Taiwan
Strait.

The interpretations of those writers who believe that there was substantial disagreement between the allies and that the Chinese were dissatisfied with the support they received from the Russians suggest that the Soviet Union exercised considerable and perhaps decisive restraint on the Chinese government before and during the crisis. The analysis of those writers who believe that there was basic agreement and mutual confidence between the parties and that the Chinese received exactly the support they wanted suggests that the Soviet Union did not find it necessary to exercise such a degree of restraining influence upon the Chinese. Both sets of interpretations rest on very limited evidence, and it is not possible today to decide with certainty which is nearer the truth. But, since Halperin's and Tsou's theory seems almost as plausible as the alternative one, it cannot be assumed here that the Soviet Union restrained China to the point of controlling its behaviour in the crisis.

Undoubtedly, even well before the crisis, there was *some* disagreement between the two powers about the general strategy to be followed in relations with the opponents. While the Chinese apparently were inclined to think that the improvement in Soviet armaments and delivery systems, manifested by the Sputnik in 1957, had changed the global balance of forces enough to make it possible for the socialist camp to resist or, in certain circumstances, even to challenge the enemy with impunity, the Russians still seemed very conscious of the danger that a military confrontation with the United States might lead to a nuclear war. This differing evaluation of the deterrent effect of Soviet arms presumably disposed the Chinese to favour a somewhat firmer general policy and a more probing strategy towards the West. In the particular issue of the offshore islands, which of course involved the Chinese far more deeply than the Russians, China obviously had much greater incentives to take risks than the Soviet Union. For these reasons it may be assumed that the Soviet leaders were more afraid than the Chinese of the possible consequences of a direct military clash with the United States in the Taiwan Strait, and were therefore anxious not to be involved in the hostilities. Signs of this attitude may be seen in the Soviet emphasis on playing a deterrent role only, which became increasingly pronounced in the later stages of the crisis, and in the apparent shunning of any physical measures of preparation for military intervention. For the same reasons it seems quite possible that the Soviet Union cautioned the Chinese government at the outset of the crisis, and even possible that it urged a rather speedier diplomatic retreat in September than the Chinese wanted. But even if the Soviet government did do so, it does not necessarily follow that it effectively restrained the Chinese in the crisis. There are signs that the Chinese leaders themselves were determined from the outset to pursue their aims with a high degree of caution, and to avoid becoming involved in a direct military clash with the United States. If this was their attitude, the Soviet Union may have done little more than simply reinforce this determination, perhaps by encouraging the Chinese to exercise particular restraint at certain junctures of the crisis.

Rather more is known about the behaviour of the United States in the crisis than about that of the Soviet Union. American relations with Nationalist China, it seems clear, were ambiguous. While on the one hand the American government went to great lengths to support the Nationalist Chinese, on the other hand it took some steps to restrain them in the clash with the Communists. Since the United States itself was deeply involved in the conflict and since it was on the side of the weaker of the two Chinas, it more often felt compelled to strengthen the hand of its client than to check its actions. American backing of Taiwan took two major forms, public statements warning Communist China and physical measures strengthening Nationalist China.

At an early stage of the crisis, after the intensification of the shelling of the offshore islands, Dulles issued a warning that, if Peking were 'to attempt to change the situation by force', it could hardly be considered 'a limited operation', the implication being that the pledges the United States had given to Taipeh might be brought into play.[6] Shortly after this statement, the American Secretary of the Army assured Nationalist troops that 'the United States will always fight shoulder to shoulder with your country for the freedom of humanity'.[7] Then, on 4 September, after consultations with President Eisenhower, Dulles issued a statement in which he said that 'the securing and protecting of Quemoy and Matsu have increasingly become related to the defence of Taiwan', and announced that the United States had made military dispositions which would enable the President to take 'timely and effective' action if he found that the employment of American armed forces was required for the defence of Taiwan.[8] After Peking had announced the extension of Chinese territorial waters from three to twelve miles, Washington took a further step by declaring that the United States would not hesitate to attack the mainland of

China if an attack on the offshore islands appeared imminent and seemed likely to be too strong for the Nationalists to deal with on their own.[9] And on 11 September President Eisenhower, in an address to the American nation, implied that the United States was fully prepared to help defend not only Taiwan and the Pescadores but also the offshore islands:

> Today, the Chinese Communists announce, repeatedly and officially, that their military operations against Quemoy are preliminary to attack on Formosa. So it is clear that the Formosa Straits resolution of 1955 applies to the present situation. If the present bombardment and harassment of Quemoy should be converted into a major assault, with which the local defenders could not cope, then we would be compelled to face precisely the situation that Congress visualized in 1955.[10]

The United States, he assured the Chinese and Soviet governments, could not be lured or frightened into 'appeasement' in the face of 'armed aggression'. Though the American administration, probably in order to maintain freedom of choice and to avoid too rigid a posture, hesitated till rather late in the crisis to commit itself decisively to the view that the offshore islands fell within the scope of the Formosa Resolution of 29 January 1955, nevertheless, through its various statements it clearly warned the opponent that the United States, if necessary, would be prepared to intervene militarily.

The physical measures aimed at strengthening Nationalist China took various forms. Having announced fairly early in the crisis that it intended to reinforce the Seventh Fleet in the Taiwan area, the American government continued building up the strength of the Fleet in September until it reached very impressive proportions. After the intensification of the bombardment of Quemoy, the Americans played a decisive part in breaking the Chinese blockade of the islands by escorting Nationalist supply vessels and giving logistic support. Furthermore, the American government supplied eight-inch howitzers to Quemoy, Sabre jets and Sidewinder air-to-air guided missiles to the Nationalist air force and ground-to-air anti-aircraft missiles for Taiwan, the effect of which was to give the Nationalists a clear superiority in the air in the clash with the Communists.

American restraint of Nationalist China became important

particularly over the issue of bombing the mainland. The Nationalists, with the idea of returning to the mainland always at the back of their minds, were generally in favour of extending the clash with the Communists and drawing the Americans into violent hostilities. Periodically throughout the crisis they attempted to make the Americans agree to bombing raids against coastal batteries opposite Quemoy, arguing that this was the only or the best way of breaking the artillery blockade. The United States, anxious to avoid becoming involved in violent exchanges with the Communists, insisted on using only non-violent means to break the blockade. In general throughout the crisis, the American government took both political and physical measures to restrain the ally from expanding the military confrontation.[11] Though the Americans never managed to establish actual control over the Nationalists, they did succeed in preventing them from bombing the mainland.

Another issue between the Americans and the Nationalists concerned the stationing of Nationalist troops on the offshore islands. It came into the open in the press conference Dulles gave on 30 September. The United States, he stated in reply to a question, had not thought it sound to make the major commitment of force to the islands that its ally had wished to make. 'In view, however, of the very strong views of the Republic of China, we were acquiescent in that. We did not attempt to veto it. The result is, I might say, one of acquiescence on the part of the United States, not of approval. Nor did we attempt to veto it after having used persuasion.' Answering another question, he said that the American government had thought it 'rather foolish' to put these large forces on the islands, and that it would not be wise or prudent, even in military terms, to keep them there if a reasonably dependable cease-fire could be brought about.[12] Chiang Kai-shek reacted strongly, declaring himself 'incredulous' at Dulles's statement. 'I doubt that his remarks could be construed to mean that he would expect us to reduce our garrison forces on the offshore islands,' he said; and even if that were the case, he added, 'it would only be a unilateral declaration and my government would be under no obligation to accept it'.[13] Two weeks later, when the Communists had suspended their bombardment of the islands and subsequently extended the cease-fire, Dulles was asked whether he intended to urge Chiang Kai-shek to reduce the strength of the forces on Quemoy. 'We have no plans whatsoever for urging him to do that', was his answer. 'I would not want to give the impression that we are pressing or plan to press the Republic of China to do something against its better judgment.'[14] Eisenhower followed up with an assurance that the United States did not intend to try to coerce its ally into changing a policy which it considered, rightly or wrongly, to be essential to its security.[15]

Many writers, especially at the time but also later on, have seen in Dulles's statements of 30 September signs of an important shift in the American position in the crisis, towards a negotiated settlement of the status of the offshore islands. But a scholar writing some ten years after the crisis has found evidence which suggests that these statements were essentially tactical moves, designed to appeal to world opinion and put forward on the safe assumption that neither of the two Chinas would consider settling the crisis by negotiating about the islands.[16] But whatever the significance of Dulles's replies and whatever the nature of the exchanges the Americans must have had with the Nationalists about the forces on the offshore islands, it seems clear that the United States never exercised a significant influence on the Nationalist government in this respect. The statements of Dulles and Eisenhower make it obvious that, even if it was seriously concerned about the presence of such large forces in that area, the American government was not prepared, either before the crisis or after the cease-fire, to try to coerce the Nationalist leaders into reducing or withdrawing their troops.

The third of the issues that played some part in relations between the two allies during the crisis, especially in its later stages, was closely tied up with the other two. It concerned the Nationalist idea of a return to the mainland. When Dulles was asked in his press conference of 30 September whether the United States expected or supported such a return, whether by force or by some other means, he answered that it was 'a highly hypothetical matter' which depended on what happened on the mainland.[17] On 10 October, however, Chiang Kai-shek reiterated his pledge to fight back to the mainland.[18] Ten days later Dulles arrived in Taipeh to have discussions with the Nationalist leaders. The joint communiqué, dated 23 October, issued after the talks, indicated that the idea of returning in force had been an important subject of discussion between the parties. The relevant passage read:

> The two governments reaffirmed their dedication to the principles of the Charter of the United Nations. They recalled that

the treaty under which they are acting is defensive in character. The Government of the Republic of China considers that the restoration of freedom to its people on the mainland is its sacred mission. It believes that the foundation of this mission resides in the minds and the hearts of the Chinese people and that the principal means of successfully achieving its mission is the implementation of Dr. Sun Yat-sen's three people's principles (nationalism, democracy and social well-being) and not the use of force.[19]

The shift of emphasis from the use of force to the implementation of Sun Yat-sen's principles as the means of achieving the sacred mission of the Nationalists suggested that the Americans had brought some influence to bear and had succeeded in imposing certain restraints on Nationalist plans. However, subsequent attempts by the Nationalists to explain away their renunciation of the use of force and to redefine their undertakings to the Americans made the position of the Nationalists on this issue highly ambiguous and cast a good deal of doubt on the success of the Americans in restraining their ally.

Though the Americans succeeded in preventing the Nationalists from bombing the mainland coasts, they neither contrived to secure a withdrawal of forces from the offshore islands nor managed to obtain an explicit renunciation of the use of force for a return to the mainland. The United States may have been neither willing nor able to exercise effective general control of its ally. A strict curbing of Nationalist conduct in the conflict was probably considered undesirable, since it could have weakened the ally in an issue in which the United States itself had a very large stake. What is more, it would have run counter to the general American policy of cautious brinkmanship in East-West crises. Most likely, such a curbing would also have been politically impossible to achieve because any attempt to coerce the Nationalists into giving way on points which they considered of crucial importance to their own efforts might well have incited them to take measures to expand the hostilities as a way of drawing the Americans into an open clash with the Communists. If some measure of agreement between the Soviet Union and Communist China about the need for caution may have made it almost unnecessary for the Russians to curb the Chinese, a fundamental disagreement between the United States and Nationalist China about the degree of caution required certainly made it very difficult for the Americans to impose severe restraints on the Nationalists.

Though the Soviet Union may have given at least some encouragement to Chinese cautiousness and the United States seems to have placed some restraint on Nationalist aggressiveness, it was not primarily through such separate efforts of the superpowers to control their clients that the crisis was managed. The real reason why war was averted and tension reduced was that the principal parties to the crisis were not the two Chinas but Communist China and the United States, and that each of these powers was anxious to avoid a violent clash with the other. The Communist Chinese, possibly having initiated the crisis as a probing operation, apparently did not want to intensify the clash once it had become clear that the United States and its ally were prepared to react forcefully. Instead of, for instance, giving orders to attack American escort vessels, their leaders took care to avoid measures which might exacerbate tension. The Americans, though they made a great show of force, were careful not to overreact to the Communist prodding. Rather than break the blockade through violence, they restrained not only the Nationalists but also themselves from taking offensive initiatives.

The crisis was settled through what Charles Osgood would call graduated reciprocation in tension-reduction. The opening move was Chou En-lai's statement of 6 September, in which he, though ostensibly taking a strong line, announced that his government was prepared to resume the ambassadorial talks between the two countries.[20] The American government reacted promptly by instructing its ambassador in Warsaw to be ready to start the talks as soon as the Chinese ambassador had returned from Peking.[21] The talks were resumed on 15 September and were continued with intervals during the rest of the crisis, though apparently with little result. The confrontation, it seems, was brought to an end not so much through negotiation as by means of gradual physical disengagement. On 6 October the Chinese Minister of National Defence sent a message to the people of Taiwan announcing that he had ordered the bombardment to be suspended immediately for a trial period of seven days, during which the Nationalists would be free to ship in supplies to the islands provided there was no American escort.[22] The Americans responded by accepting this stipulation on the condition that the Chinese Communists did not make it necessary for them to escort Nationalist supply vessels. The next Chinese step, which followed on 13 October, was to extend the suspension of bombardment for another two weeks. Though the shelling was resumed briefly on 20 October, presumably to coincide with Dulles's arrival in Taipeh, the crisis was by then in the process of liquidation. By the end of the month, although neither the issue between the two Chinas nor that between Communist China and the United States had been settled or even seriously tackled, tension between the parties had been reduced to pre-crisis level.

Joint or concerted efforts by the superpowers to control the course of events were not a feature of this crisis. Relations between the Soviet Union and the United States were so unfriendly and contact between them so minimal that the possibility of coordinating their attempts to influence events barely existed. The United States throughout treated the Soviet Union with the greatest suspicion and concentrated on its confrontation with the CPR. The Soviet Union, as already explained, took care to remain behind the scenes in the earlier major stage of the crisis. Apart from releasing a few statements on Moscow Radio and in the Soviet press attacking the brinkmanship of Dulles and displaying its loyalty to Communist China, the Soviet Union up till 6 September avoided all acts and utterances of a challenging or threatening kind. But in the second stage of the crisis the Soviet government initiated a bitter exchange of messages with the American President.

On 7 September Khrushchev sent Eisenhower a long, rambling letter, which was mainly about the situation in the Far East.[23] He attacked the United States in rather sharp terms for its policies towards China and Taiwan and its conduct of international relations in general, warned about the consequent risk to world peace, and called upon the American government to show reasonableness. The United States, he complained, was striving to assume the functions of some kind of world gendarme in the Taiwan Straits area. The movement of its naval and military forces could be regarded only as 'a direct provocation'. After strongly criticising the United States for its general practice of dispatching warships to any part of the world, he suggested that the heyday of surface navy power had passed with the advent of nuclear and rocket weapons. Moving on to deal with certain threats to China made in statements by various American political and military leaders, Khrushchev insisted that attempts to resort to atomic blackmail against other countries were utterly hopeless in present circumstances, 'with the

United States having lost the monopoly of atomic arms'. In two other passages he warned about the possibility of Soviet intervention. China was not alone, he emphasised, but had 'true friends who are ready to come to its aid at any moment in the event of an act of aggression against China, because the security interests of People's China are inseparable from those of the Soviet Union'. If the United States believed it could make short work of China, its miscalculation would have grave consequences for the cause of world peace. 'An attack on the Chinese People's Republic, which is a great friend, ally and neighbour of our country, is an attack on the Soviet Union. Loyal to its duty, our country would do everything to defend, jointly with People's China, the security of both countries and the interests of peace in the Far East and throughout the rest of the world.' Though the three passages did not appear consecutively, taken together and seen against the background of Khrushchev's observations on the strategic importance of nuclear and rocket weapons, they may be read as implying a threat of atomic war.

Khrushchev denied that he wished to lay the colour on too thickly or that he intended to make threats. All he wanted to do was to find a common language with the American government 'so as to end the present downward movement and so that the USSR, the United States, the Chinese People's Republic and other countries may join efforts in removing the tension which has now arisen in the Far East, and so that one could say that a good job for world peace had been done by combined efforts'. In closing his message, which he said was 'dictated by the awareness of the great responsibility which our countries bear for safeguarding world peace', he stressed that it completely depended on the future actions of the United States government whether peace could prevail in the Far East.

In President Eisenhower's address to the nation of 11 September, already referred to,[24] he mentioned the letter he had received from Khrushchev and indicated what his answer would be. Pointing to the danger that 'aggression by ruthless despots' again presented to the United States and to the free world, he observed that the Chinese Communists and the Soviet Union appeared to be working hand in hand in this effort. Khrushchev's warning to the United States not to help its allies in the Western Pacific and to return its naval forces to the home bases, Eisenhower implied, was designed to leave America's friends in the Far East to face alone the combined military powers of the Soviet Union and Communist China. 'Does

Mr. Khrushchev think that we have so soon forgotten Korea?' he asked.

Eisenhower's formal answer to Khrushchev's message came in a letter of 12 September.[25] Taking issue with Khrushchev about the source of danger in the Taiwan area, the President argued that the existing state of tension had resulted from the Chinese Communists' sudden initiation of heavy artillery bombardment of Quemoy, which, he did not fail to point out, had been undertaken some three weeks after Khrushchev's visit to Peking. Khrushchev's description of the role of the United States in the cirsis was an 'upside down presentation' of the facts. Turning to the future, the President said that the American government had welcomed the willingness of the Chinese Communists to resume talks in the hope that an understanding could be reached which would preclude the use of force in the area. But, he suggested, Khrushchev's call for a search for a common language and for initiation of joint efforts to remove tension did not carry conviction:

> I regret to say [the President wrote in the penultimate paragraph of his letter] I do not see in your letter any effort to find that common language which could indeed facilitate the removal of the danger existing in the current situation in the Taiwan area. On the contrary, the description of this situation contained in your letter seems designed to serve the ambitions of international Communism rather than to present the facts. I also note that you have addressed no letter to the Chinese Communist leaders urging moderation upon them. If your letter to me is not merely a vehicle for one-sided denunciation of United States actions but is indeed intended to reflect a desire to find a common language for peace, I suggest you urge these leaders to discontinue their military operations and to turn to a policy of peaceful settlement of the Taiwan dispute.

Khrushchev's rejoinder, dated a week later, was considerably sharper than his first letter.[26] Much of its was devoted to defending the legality of the Communist government of the Chinese People's Republic and to attacking the relations of the United States government with 'the Chiang Kai-shek clique'. Taking up the last point made in Eisenhower's letter, Khrushchev said that he had addressed his earlier message to the President and not to the government of the CPR for the simple reason that it was not China which was interfering in the internal affairs of the United States but the United States which had grossly interfered in China's affairs. To urge the Soviet government to exert influence on the Chinese government in connection with the Taiwan events meant trying to induce the Soviet Union to interfere in China's domestic affairs. 'The Soviet Union would never be a party to such a shameful affair, as that would be fundamentally contrary to its peaceful foreign policy and would be incompatible with the relationship of unbreakable friendship and fraternal co-operation between the Soviet and the Chinese peoples.' Had the Soviet government agreed with the American point of view, he continued, it would, in fact, have been contributing to the preparations for a war against China, which was an utterly absurd idea.

Turning to press reports that American air force units equipped with nuclear weapons had been rushed to Taiwan together with rockets and guided missiles, Khrushchev pointed out that such actions tended 'to aggravate the situation and increase the danger of an outbreak of war involving the use of the most devastating modern weapons'. Atomic blackmail, however, would intimidate neither the Soviet Union nor the CPR. 'Those who harbour plans for an atomic attack on the Chinese People's Republic should not forget that the other side too has atomic and hydrogen weapons and the appropriate means to deliver them, and if the Chinese People's Republic falls victim to such an attack, the aggressor will at once suffer a rebuff by the same means.' This invocation of the nuclear deterrent was emphasised by a later passage in which Khrushchev stressed again that 'an attack on the Chinese People's Republic is an attack on the Soviet Union' and insisted that the Soviet Union would not fail to meet its commitments under the Sino-Soviet Treaty. Having warned Eisenhower that to touch off a war against China would mean to ignite the conflagration of a world war, for which the responsibility would rest with the President personally, Khrushchev once more appealed to him not to bring the atmosphere to red heat. The governments, above all the governments of their two countries, he declared, were duty bound to do everything necessary to ensure peaceful cooperation among states. To this end the United States should stop supporting the Chiang Kai-shek clique and should recognise the government of the Chinese People's Republic.

The United States rejected this letter on the grounds that it was offensive and out of order and returned it to the Soviet government.

White House statements of 20 September described Khrushchev's message as 'abusive and intemperate'.[27] A subsequent TASS statement expressed Soviet resentment at having the letter returned by saying that the step taken by the United States government showed the unwillingness of the American ruling circles to heed the voice of reason.[28]

This exchange of public messages, marked as it was by increasing bitterness and hostility, hardly showed signs of the superpowers moving closer to each other in the later stages of the crisis. Whether or not the Soviet calls for a common language and joint efforts were more than propaganda aimed at world public opinion, they were not taken up by the United States. Similarly, the American appeal to the Soviet government to pacify the Chinese Communists, which had an equally slim chance of meeting with a favourable response, was rejected by the Soviet Union. Nor does there seem to be any evidence on the diplomatic level of concerted initiatives between the two powers. A third point of contact was the United Nations, but this again does not appear to have been used for coordinating attempts by the Soviet Union and the United States to influence the course of events in the Far East. For a variety of reasons—including the non-membership of the CPR, the unwillingness of the Chinese to recognise the right of this organisation to deal with their affairs, the preoccupation of the General Assembly with events in the Middle East, and the American reluctance to bring the crisis before the world forum—the United Nations played only a marginal role in the crisis. Both Gromyko and Dulles dealt with the issue in speeches in the General Assembly; but the main function of the United Nations was probably to provide a forum for private conversations between the representatives of the two powers. It is known that Dulles and Gromyko dined with Hammarskjöld in New York on 27 September,[29] but not what they discussed, nor whether they reached any agreement. On no level of communication between the Soviet Union and the United States is there clear evidence that the two powers at any stage attempted to concert their efforts to manage the crisis.

Nevertheless, separately, the superpowers, as we have seen, took various measures to avert war and reduce tension. These may be divided into four sets. First, the Soviet Union and the United States in all probability encouraged their Chinese allies to exercise caution at certain junctures of the crisis or urged them to accept restraint in particular respects. Second, each of the superpowers called on the adversary to control its ally. When Khrushchev, after 6 September, drew attention to the possibility of premeditated action by the Nationalists, he seemed to be warning the United States to keep a tight rein on the force of Nationalist China in order to forestall Chiang Kai-shek from triggering a conflict between the Soviet Union and the United States.[30] Eisenhower, on his part, suggested to Khrushchev that he urge the Communist Chinese leaders to give up their military operations and to work for a peaceful settlement. Third, each of the superpowers exercised a good deal of self-restraint. This was most conspicuous in the case of the Soviet Union, which in the earlier stages kept out of the conflict and throughout refrained from taking physical measures to influence the course of events. But the United States, too, displayed considerable control, first in its non-violent reactions to the blockade and then in its response to Chinese steps to reduce tension. Fourth, each of the superpowers found a way of hinting or threatening some form of retaliation in order to prevent the other side from escalating the crisis. Some of the statements made in the earlier stage of the crisis by prominent military and civilian Americans below the level of President and Secretary of State, together with the shipment of certain arms to Taiwan, suggested that the United States was prepared to respond with whatever force was deemed necessary to stop Chinese aggression, even with small-size nuclear weapons. And in the later stage of the crisis the Soviet Union, particularly through Khrushchev's second letter, openly invoked the nuclear deterrent. Unlike the American implied threat, which portended only a limited use of nuclear weapons and was aimed in the first place at the Chinese Communists, the Russian threat foreshadowed a more extensive employment of such weapons and was aimed directly at the United States.

The four types of measures were not equally important in influencing the course and outcome of the crisis. Attempts to restrain the allies appear on the whole to have been, on one side, perhaps not strictly necessary and, on the other, not particularly successful. Yet the Soviet Union probably did caution and possibly even marginally restrain Communist China at crucial junctures, particularly in the later stages of the crisis. And the United States did succeed in the important task of preventing Nationalist China from bombing the mainland. The appeals of each superpower to the other to control its ally had little effect, partly because they seemed to be made largely for propaganda purposes, which made it difficult for the adversary to respond positively, and partly because each power was already doing what it considered necessary, desirable, or possible in that respect. The exercise of self-restraint on behalf of both of the powers was, of course, of the greatest importance in localising the crisis and averting a general war. The various hints or threats of retaliation, however, seem to have been of little consequence, probably essentially because all the three major powers were determined anyway to exercise caution and prevent escalation.

In so far as the crisis was managed at all by the superpowers, it was done primarily through self-control and only secondarily by restraining the local participants. For two dominant powers to help prevent an international crisis from developing into world war mainly by either not becoming involved or taking care not to overreact represents dual crisis management reduced to a minimum, especially when in each case such self-restraint is accompanied by diplomatic or physical actions designed to outflank the adversary. The clash in the Taiwan Strait in 1958 was a typical cold-war encounter. Facing each other in hostility, the superpowers kept up a bitter rivalry but exerted their pressure on each other through proxies rather than directly and used bluff and threats instead of open violence.

A shared concern to avoid nuclear war made the superpower rivals engage in separate efforts to limit the conflict. But the idea of carrying a joint responsibility for the conduct of world politics and the maintenance of international order does not seem to have guided the Soviet Union and the United States in their behaviour and interaction in this crisis. Though the confrontation was overcome, the underlying issue was left untouched. Both powers clearly preferred to let the situation in the Far East remain in a state which would allow them to continue their rivalry in the region.

3 Cuba 1962

Unlike the two earlier situations of conflict considered here, the Cuban missile crisis was a direct confrontation between the United States and the Soviet Union. Though the underlying issue involved Cuba and its relations with each of the superpowers, that country played a role only in the initial phase and in the closing stages of the crisis. While the outcome of the confrontation had serious repercussions in the relationship between China and the Soviet Union, China seems to have taken no part in the crisis until the final stage and then only a very minor one. At the height of the conflict, the Soviet Union and the United States occupied the stage alone, facing each other as the unchallenged leaders of hostile blocs.

Since the concern here, as in the analysis of the two earlier crises, is with the interaction of the United States and the Soviet Union during the clash itself, it is reasonable to ignore the origins of the confrontation of October 1962. There is no need to discuss whether the missiles were installed on the suggestion of the Russians or, as Castro occasionally claimed later on, at the request of the Cuban government. Nor is it necessary to consider whether the Soviet motives for offering or agreeing to place missiles on Cuban territory were simply to prevent an American invasion, as Khrushchev insisted at a late stage of the crisis and subsequently repeated, or primarily to improve the bargaining position of the Soviet Union in the issue over Berlin, as American leaders feared at the time, or indeed mainly to strengthen the Soviet position in the global balance of power, as some Western writers since have suggested.[1]

For the same reason, we can pay only passing attention to the earlier phase of the crisis, in which the superpowers did not yet share the knowledge of having a major conflict on their hands. Not until 22 October, when the Americans suddenly and publicly made it clear to the Russians that they knew what was happening in Cuba and intended to put an end to it, was it evident to both of the powers that they had to deal with a serious confrontation. But, expedient though it is to start with the opening of the acute stage of the crisis, it is necessary to carry the analysis well beyond the end of this stage.

The closing phases of the crisis, in which some writers have detected elements of 'condominium' in the way in which the superpowers imposed their agreement on the Cubans, must be included in this study. Thus, the focus will be on the period between the date when the superpowers entered into confrontation and the less well-defined point in time when most of the terms in the settlement had been implemented.

In this period, the parties interacted in three different ways: by maintaining confrontation, by conducting negotiations, and by implementing the agreement. The first two processes were intertwined. No sooner had the powers found themselves face to face in a hostile clash than they started to search for a way of averting war and 'normalising' their relations. The third process was a product of the others. The tension of confrontation was at least as important as the spirit of negotiation in producing a settlement. While the confrontation and the negotiation took place strictly between the superpowers, the implementation of the agreement involved Cuba too. It will be convenient to examine first the dualistic relationship of confrontation and negotiation and then the tripartite process of implementation.

The confrontation between Washington and Moscow took place partly in the United Nations and partly on the high seas round Cuba. The clash in the United Nations was by far the less important. In the context of the crisis, the proceedings of the Security Council on 23, 24 and 25 October were merely a 'side show', which allowed the United States to present its case to the world and the Soviet Union to gain a little extra time for completing its installations in Cuba. After President Kennedy's address to the American nation on 22 October, Adlai Stevenson, the permanent representative of the United States at the United Nations, requested an urgent meeting of the Security Council to deal with 'the dangerous threat to the peace and security of the world caused by the secret establishment in Cuba by the Union of Soviet Socialist Republics of launching bases and the installation of long-range ballistic missiles capable of carrying thermonuclear warheads to most of North and South America'. The purpose of Security Council action, he said in his letter, should be to bring about the immediate dismantling and withdrawal of the Soviet missiles and other offensive weapons, under United Nations supervision, so as to make it possible to lift the quarantine which the American government was imposing. The United States, he declared, was willing to confer with the Soviet Union on measures to remove the threat to the security of the West and the peace of the world.[2] A draft resolution along these lines was attached to his letter.

The Soviet delegate replied with a lengthy and belligerent statement, which was accompanied by a rival draft resolution. The United States, it declared, was pushing the world towards the abyss of military catastrophe, and the Soviet government considered it its duty to address a serious warning to the American government. The United States was in no position to force its dispositions on other states, because it was no longer the greatest power on the world scene. There was another and no less powerful force in the world. However, Soviet nuclear weapons would never be used for aggressive purposes. 'But if the aggressors unleash war, the Soviet Union will inflict the most powerful blow in response.'[3] The draft resolution condemned the American blockade, insisted on its revocation, proposed an end to United States interference in the internal affairs of Cuba and called upon the United States, the People's Republic of China and the Soviet Union to enter into negotiations so as to bring the situation back to normal.[4]

When the two protagonists had drawn up their positions, the initiative fell to the Secretary General. At the request of Ghana and the United Arab Republic, U Thant addressed identical letters to Chairman Khrushchev and President Kennedy, urgently appealing to them to refrain from any action which might aggravate the situation and suggesting, on the one hand, a voluntary suspension of arms shipments to Cuba and, on the other, a voluntary suspension of the quarantine measures long enough to allow the parties to meet and discuss ways of solving the problem peacefully. He also offered to make himself available if he could be of any help.[5]

While Khrushchev accepted U Thant's recommendation,[6] Kennedy reiterated that the answer to the existing threat lay in the removal of the offensive weapons, but said that Stevenson was ready to enter into discussions.[7] Further appeals from U Thant for the issue of instructions aimed at avoiding physical confrontation on the seas were accepted by both leaders. Next followed the celebrated clash between the representatives of the two powers in the Security Council, with Stevenson presenting photographic evidence and demanding a clear answer to his question about the presence of Soviet missiles in Cuba and Zorin replying that he was not in an American court of law. This was the end of the Security Council's part in the crisis. Having made no progress at all in dealing with the conflict, it adjourned on 25 October, not to meet again till the crisis was over. After that date, the role of the United Nations was limited to providing informal contact between the opponents, direct between their representatives in New York and indirect through the Secretary General.

The real clash of the superpowers took place directly between Washington and Moscow. In his address to the American nation in the evening of 22 October, President Kennedy announced the discovery that offensive missile sites were being prepared and jet bombers capable of carrying nuclear weapons were being uncrated and assembled in Cuba. The 'secret, swift, and extraordinary buildup of Communist missiles', he said, was 'a deliberately provocative and unjustified change in the status quo' which could not be accepted by the United States. Listing a number of steps he was going to take to secure the withdrawal or elimination of the missiles, he emphasised that they were only initial measures. The first was a strict 'quarantine' on all offensive military equipment under shipment to Cuba and the second an increase in the close surveillance of Cuba accompanied by preparation for action to deal with a further military buildup. Thirdly, he declared that it should be the policy of the United States 'to regard any nuclear missile launched from Cuba against any nation in the Western Hemisphere as an attack by the Soviet Union on the United States, requiring a full retaliatory response upon the Soviet Union'. He also called on Khrushchev to abandon the course of world domination and to join in an effort to end the arms race and 'move the world back from the abyss of destruction'. Finally, he warned that any hostile movement elsewhere in the world, including Berlin, would be met by whatever action was needed.[8]

An hour before the speech, Secretary Rusk had broken the news of the blockade to the Soviet Ambassador in Washington. The following day the President issued a formal proclamation announcing that the blockade would take effect on the next day, 24 October.[9] The same evening Robert Kennedy called on the Soviet Ambassador to relate to him the serious implications of the crisis which had arisen as a result of the Russian installation of missiles in Cuba.

Despite the firm, public demand for a withdrawal of the missiles, the threatening language in the President's speech and the serious warnings delivered privately to Dobrynin, the American reaction to the Soviet initiative in Cuba evinced some caution and restraint, both in the choice of measures and in their execution. A blockade of Cuba, which had been decided on by the group of presidential advisers, acting under the title of the Executive Committee of the National Security Council, after prolonged and intensive discussion, had the advantage over the two principal alternatives considered, namely an air strike and an invasion; it did not necessarily involve violence and therefore was less likely to provoke the Soviet government to retaliate. The delay with which it was imposed gave the Russians time to consider their position carefully before deciding how to react. Furthermore, the decision to move the blockade line closer to Cuba, taken on 24 October, and the orders to American captains to delay intercepting ships as long as possible served to postpone the moment of physical confrontation and thus to give the opponent additional time to seek a way of avoiding violence. At the outset of the acute stage of the crisis, American policy was to combine threats of violent action with firm but non-violent measures.

At this early stage of the confrontation, the Soviet line, too, was to mix threats of violence with caution in action. The verbal reaction to the blockade was rather aggressive. Having returned as unacceptable the US note announcing the imposition of the blockade, Khrushchev found various unusual ways of threatening the Americans with violent action. In a conversation he arranged with the American businessman William Knox on 24 October, he apparently talked vaguely about the use of missiles and about the role submarines might play in breaking the blockade.[10] In his letter to Bertrand Russell of the same day, he said that if the American government carried out the programme of piratic actions it had outlined, the Soviet government would have to resort to means of defence to protect its rights against the aggressor.[11] Other warnings were sent to the Americans that specific acts of violence would be met with massive retaliation.[12]

Even some of these messages, however, indicated that Khrushchev was anxious to avoid violence. In the letter to Bertrand Russell, for example, he stated that his government would do everything possible to prevent a catastrophe, and suggested that a summit meeting might be useful.[13] Khrushchev's attitude of restraint was even more conspicuous in his actions. He not only refrained from using submarines or resorting to other means of breaking the blockade but also, on the day of his meeting with Knox and his letter to Russell, gave orders for at least twelve Russian ships which were on their way to Cuba to be halted.

It does seem, however, that Khrushchev's motive in exercising so much self-control in the field was not merely to avoid any sort of violence which might lead to war but also to gain time to complete the construction of the missile sites in Cuba. The American discovery of this project before it had reached completion had put him at a serious tactical disadvantage in the confrontation and had given him good reason to postpone any clash between Russian and American ships until the Soviet Union had established itself more firmly in the area. Thus, his order to halt the ships, like his acceptance of U Thant's request and Zorin's denials in the Security Council, could be seen largely as delaying-tactics. At any rate, while Zorin engaged in rhetoric in the United Nations and Khrushchev exercised caution in the field, the construction of missile sites continued apace in Cuba.

The fact that it was possible for the Russian technicians, working with materials already in Cuba, to continue the preparation of missile sites reduced the effectiveness of the blockade as a weapon in the conflict and encouraged the United States to resort to other means of putting pressure on the Soviet Union. In their maintenance of the blockade, the Americans still exercised the greatest care not to cause any offence to the Russians which might invite a violent response. Thus, with a minimum of fuss they let through several Soviet or Soviet-chartered ships which carried inoffensive cargoes. But in other directions they moved closer to violent hostilities. The President, pursuing his policy of a gradual increase in pressure, ordered not only a stepping-up of the reconnaissance flights over Cuba and an extension of the embargo list but also the preparations of detailed plans for invasion and occupation of Cuba. On the 26th, the White House issued a statement reporting that the development of the offensive missile sites in Cuba was continuing at a rapid pace and that there were no signs of any intention to dismantle or discontinue the constructions.[14] Warnings that invasion was imminent went out to NATO allies; and Robert Kennedy told the Soviet Ambassador that the President could hold his hand for no more than another two days.

While all this was happening, President Kennedy and Mr Khrushchev were in daily communication by letter.[15] The President opened the exchange on the 22nd with a message in which he underlined the determination of the United States to stand up to its opponent:

In our discussions and exchanges on Berlin and other international questions, the one thing that has most concerned me
has been the possibility that your Government would not
correctly understand the will and determination of the United
States in any given situation, since I have not assumed that you or
any other sane man would, in this nuclear age, deliberately
plunge the world into war which it is crystal clear no country
could win and which could only result in catastrophic consequences to the whole world, including the aggressor.[16]

Khrushchev answered by accusing the United States of grossly
violating both the Charter of the United Nations and international
norms of freedom of navigation on the high seas and of taking the
path of aggression against Cuba and the Soviet Union. Refusing to
recognise any right of the United States to establish control over
armaments essential for the defence of Cuba, he expressed the hope
that the American government would show prudence and renounce
its actions. In a brief reply, dated the 23rd, Kennedy asked
Khrushchev to arrange for the terms of the quarantine to be
observed. He was concerned, he said, that both parties 'show
prudence and do nothing to allow events to make the situation more
difficult to control than it already is'.[17]

The following day Khrushchev despatched a message in which he
declared that Soviet vessels would not observe the blockade.
Accusing Kennedy of threatening the Soviet Union, he asserted that
the actions of the United States constituted 'outright banditry', or
'the folly of degenerate imperialism', and pushed mankind 'towards
the abyss of a world missile-nuclear war'. If the Americans violated
the generally recognised norms of navigation in international
waters and engaged in piratical actions against Soviet ships, his
government would be forced to take the measures it deemed
necessary and adequate in order to protect its rights. 'For this we
have all that is necessary', he concluded.[18]

Kennedy replied by a letter of 25 October, in which he justified
the American actions by reviewing the Soviet record of wilfully
misleading the United States about the missile bases in Cuba. 'I ask
you to recognize clearly, Mr Chairman, that it was not I who issued
the first challenge in this case, and that in the light of this record
these activities in Cuba required the responses I have announced.'
Expressing his regret that these events should cause a deterioration
in relations between the two powers, he added 'I hope that your

Government will take the necessary action to permit a restoration of
the earlier situation'.[19]

On the following day John Scali, the American journalist, and
Alexander Fomin, a Soviet Counsellor in the Washington embassy
reputed to be a high intelligence officer, had their first meeting. This
contact, which was initiated by Fomin and was maintained for a
couple of days, seems to have been used by the Russians for testing
American reactions to various ideas for settling the crisis and by the
Americans for impressing on the Russians the urgency of the matter.
Khrushchev's famous letter to Kennedy of 26 October should
probably be seen as complementary to these informal talks.

Robert Kennedy correctly described this letter as very long and
emotional, pointing out that the emotion was directed at the death,
destruction and anarchy that a nuclear war would bring. The
message was important because it showed the first signs of a
willingness to negotiate a removal of the missiles in Cuba. In an
obvious reference to the impending elections in the United States,
Khrushchev warned against succumbing to 'intoxication and petty
passions'. The American government, he said, was wrong in
thinking that the Soviet means on Cuba were offensive. They were
there for defensive purposes only and could never be used to attack
the United States:

> You can regard us with distrust, but, in any case, you can be calm
> in this regard, that we are of sound mind and understand
> perfectly well that if we attack you, you will respond the same
> way. But you too will receive the same that you hurl against us.
> And I think that you also understand this. . . .
> This indicates that we are normal people, that we correctly
> understand and correctly evaluate the situation. Consequently,
> how can we permit the incorrect actions which you ascribe to us?
> Only lunatics or suicides, who themselves want to perish and to
> destroy the whole world before they die, could do this.

Despite ideological and other differences, the Soviet Union did not
want to destroy the United States but to compete peacefully.

There was no reason, he suggested, for the Americans to interfere
with any of the ships now bound for Cuba, for they carried no
weapons. All the shipments of weapons were already within Cuba,
he explained, thus implicitly acknowledging the presence of missiles
in Cuba. The reason why the Soviet government had given military

and economic aid to Cuba was that the United States wanted to overthrow the Cuban government. The Soviet Union wished to help Cuba protect itself. Then came the crucial passages:

> If assurances were given by the President and the government of the United States that the USA itself would not participate in an attack on Cuba and would restrain others from actions of this sort, if you would recall your fleet, this would immediately change everything. I am not speaking for Fidel Castro, but I think that he and the government of Cuba, evidently, would declare demobilization and would appeal to the people to get down to peaceful labor. Then, too, the question of armaments would disappear, since, if there is no threat, then armaments are a burden for every people. Then, too, the question of the destruction, not only of the armaments which you call offensive, but of all other armaments as well, would look different.
>
> I spoke in the name of the Soviet government in the United Nations and introduced a proposal for the disbandment of all armies and for the destruction of all armaments. How then can I now count on those armaments?
>
> Armaments bring only disasters. When one accumulates them, this damages the economy, and if one puts them to use, then they destroy people on both sides. Consequently, only a madman can believe that armaments are the principal means in the life of society. No, they are an enforced loss of human energy, and what is more are for the destruction of man himself. If people do not show wisdom, then in the final analysis they will come to a clash, like blind moles, and then reciprocal extermination will begin.
>
> Let us therefore show statesmanlike wisdom. I propose: we, for our part, will declare that our ships, bound for Cuba, will not carry any kind of armaments. You would declare that the United States will not invade Cuba with its forces and will not support any sort of forces which might intend to carry out an invasion of Cuba. Then the necessity for the presence of our military specialists in Cuba would disappear.
>
> Mr President, I appeal to you to weigh well what the aggressive, piratical actions, which you have declared the USA intends to carry out in international waters, would lead to. You yourself know that any sensible man simply cannot agree with this, cannot recognize your right to such actions.
>
> If you did this as the first step towards the unleashing of war,

well then, it is evident that nothing else is left to us but to accept this challenge of yours. If, however, you have not lost your self-control and sensibly conceive what this might lead to, then, Mr President, we and you ought not now to pull on the ends of the rope in which you have tied the knot of war, because the more the two of us pull, the tighter that knot will be tied. And a moment may come when that knot will be tied so tight that even he who tied it will not have the strength to untie it, and then it will be necessary to cut that knot. And what that would mean is not for me to explain to you, because you yourself understand perfectly of what terrible forces our countries dispose.

Consequently, if there is no intention to tighten that knot and thereby to doom the world to the catastrophe of thermonuclear war, then let us not only relax the forces pulling on the ends of the rope, let us take measures to untie that knot. We are ready for this.[20]

While the President and his advisers were considering how to answer this letter, a new and much more formal message from Khrushchev to Kennedy arrived in Washington. This communication contained a proposal for a settlement of the crisis rather different from that indicated in the other letter. Khrushchev was now suggesting that the United States should evacuate its rocket weapons in Turkey in return for the Soviet Union removing its weapons in Cuba. In both cases, the removal should be supervised by representatives of the United Nations Security Council, who would perform their functions with the permission of the governments of Cuba and Turkey. Secondly, the Soviet Union should pledge itself not to interfere in the internal affairs of Turkey, not to invade it, and not to make its own territory available as a *place d'armes* for such an invasion. The United States should make the same pledge with regard to Cuba. After indicating how such an agreement could be negotiated, and after pointing out that the Soviet missiles in Cuba did not threaten anyone as long as there was no invasion of Cuba, nor any attack on the Soviet Union or any of its allies, he concluded the letter in the following terms:

Why should I like to achieve this [solving the present problem]? Because the entire world is now agitated and expects from us reasonable actions. The greatest joy for all the peoples would be an announcement on our agreement, on the conflict that has arisen being nipped in the bud. I attach great importance to such an understanding, because it might be a good beginning and, in particular, might facilitate a nuclear test ban agreement. The problem of tests could be solved simultaneously, not linking one problem with the other, because they are different problems. Yet it is important to reach an understanding on both these problems in order to make a good gift to the peoples, to let them rejoice at the news that a nuclear test ban agreement has also been reached and thus there will be no further contamination of the atmosphere. Your position and our own on this issue are very close.

All this, possibly, would serve as a good impetus towards searching for mutually acceptable agreements on other disputed issues, too, on which views are being exchanged between us. These problems have not yet been solved, but they await an urgent solution which would clear the international atmosphere. We are ready for this.[21]

There has been a good deal of speculation about the connection between these two letters from Khrushchev. Robert Kennedy was certain that, while the first letter was written by Khrushchev personally, the second was the work of the Soviet Foreign Ministry. One writer has reported that some who had seen the note received first suggested that it was actually sent last and was written behind the back of the Presidium.[22] Another writer has put forward the view that a strong negative reaction from Castro to the deal outlined in the Scali-Fomin talks caused Khrushchev to change his mind and adopt the stiffer attitude of his more formal note.[23] There is no need here to consider the various possible explanations. What matters is how the Americans reacted to the two letters. The idea of a missile swap, though from some points of view hardly unreasonable,[24] was unacceptable to the United States. To withdraw the missiles in Turkey under pressure would not only have encouraged the Russians in later situations to seek political gains by initiating international crisis but might also have had repercussions in relations with the NATO allies, especially Turkey. Accordingly, the first American answer, a brief statement issued by the White House on the 27th, stated that the position of the United States was that work on the bases in Cuba must stop, offensive weapons be rendered inoperable and further shipments cease before any proposal could be considered.[25] In the meantime the 'Ex-Comm', as the committee of advisers has come to be known, was still considering how the

President should answer Khrushchev's letters.

Robert Kennedy considered this day the most difficult twenty-four hours of the crisis. When reports came in that one U-2 reconnaissance plane had been shot down over Cuba and another had strayed over Soviet territory, tension reached a climax, but was kept under control when each power decided not to retaliate. This was the situation in which Robert Kennedy thought up the move that has become known as the 'Trollope ploy'. His idea was that the President in his answer should more or less ignore the stiffer of the two letters from Khrushchev and take up those of the Soviet proposals advanced in the other letter and in the Fomin-Scali talks which suited the Americans. Having gained acceptance in the 'Ex-Comm', this suggestion found expression in the President's letter of 27 October, which read:

I have read your letter of October 26th with great care and welcomed the statement of your desire to seek a prompt solution to the problem. The first thing that needs to be done, however, is for work to cease on offensive missile bases in Cuba and for all weapons systems in Cuba capable of offensive use to be rendered inoperable, under effective United Nations arrangements.

Assuming this is done promptly, I have given my representatives in New York instructions that will permit them to work out this weekend—in cooperation with the Acting Secretary General and your representative—an arrangement for a permanent solution to the Cuban problem along the lines suggested in your letter of October 26th. As I read your letter, the key elements of your proposals—which seem generally acceptable as I understand them are as follows.

1. You would agree to remove these weapons systems from Cuba under appropriate United Nations observation and supervision; and undertake, with suitable safeguards, to halt the further introduction of such weapons systems into Cuba.

2. We, on our part, would agree—upon the establishment of adequate arrangements through the United Nations to ensure the carrying out and continuation of these commitments—(a) to remove promptly the quarantine measures now in effect and (b) to give assurances against an invasion of Cuba. I am confident that other nations of the Western Hemisphere would be prepared to do likewise.

If you will give your representative similar instructions, there is no reason why we should not be able to complete these arrangements and announce them to the world within a couple of days. The effect of such a settlement on easing world tensions would enable us to work toward a more general arrangement regarding 'other armaments', as proposed in your second letter which you made public. I would like to say again that the United States is very much interested in reducing tensions and halting the arms race; and if your letter signifies that you are prepared to discuss a détente affecting NATO and the Warsaw Pact, we are quite prepared to consider with our allies any useful proposals.

But the first ingredient, let me emphasize, is the cessation of work on missile sites in Cuba and measures to render such weapons inoperable, under effective international guarantees. The continuation of this threat, or a prolonging of this discussion concerning Cuba by linking these problems to the broader questions of European and world security, would surely lead to an intensification of the Cuban crisis and a grave risk to the peace of the world. For this reason I hope we can quickly agree along the lines outlined in this letter and in your letter of October 26th.[26]

The same evening Robert Kennedy warned the Soviet ambassador that unless the American government had a commitment by the following morning that the Russians would remove their bases in Cuba, the Americans would do it themselves. On the question of the Turkish bases, Kennedy said that there could be no *quid pro quo* under such threat or pressure, but indicated that the United States would remove those bases soon after the crisis was over. About the same time the President recalled twenty-four troop-carrier squadrons of the Air Force Reserve to active duty—a clear sign that an invasion of Cuba was imminent.

The following morning, 28 October, Khrushchev's agreement, which was broadcast in Moscow, reached Washington. After a few opening remarks came the crucial passage:

So as to eliminate as rapidly as possible the conflict which is endangering peace, to reassure all the peoples who crave for peace, and to reassure the people of America—who, I am sure, also want peace, as do the peoples of the Soviet Union—the Soviet government, in addition to the earlier instructions to cease further work on the weapon construction sites, has given a new order to dismantle those arms which you have described as offensive, to crate them and return them to the Soviet Union.

The reason why the Soviet Union had given economic assistance and also arms to Cuba, he asserted, was that that country was constantly under the threat of invasion. The means of defence had been supplied only to prevent an attack on Cuba.

I regard with respect and confidence the statement you have made in your message of October 27, 1962, that there will be no attack and no invasion of Cuba—neither by the United States, nor, as you have said in the same message, by other nations of the western hemisphere. In that situation, the motives which persuaded us to give Cuba assistance of that kind disappear.

The Soviet government was ready to reach an agreement to enable representatives of the United Nations to check up on the dismantling of the facilities provided to Cuba. Thus every condition, he observed, now existed for eliminating the conflict.

Moving to the international situation in general, Khrushchev touched on the role that the superpowers might play in other crises:

Invested, therefore, with trust and great responsibility, we must not allow the situation to become more acute and must stamp out centres where a dangerous situation, fraught with grave consequences to peace, has arisen. And if we—together with you, and with the help of other people of good will—succeed in ending this tense atmosphere, we should also make sure that no other dangerous conflicts would arise which could lead to a world nuclear catastrophe.

After stating that the Soviet government was willing to exchange views on a détente between NATO and the Warsaw Treaty countries, on the prohibition of nuclear weapons and on general disarmament, he went on to talk about the Soviet desire for peace. Violations of Soviet territory by American reconnaissance planes, a subject which he dealt with in some detail, constituted a serious danger to world peace. Violations of Cuban air space, too, could have dangerous consequences, and he appealed to the President to put a stop to this practice. He concluded his message by stating that Kuznetsov, First Deputy Foreign Minister of the Soviet Union, had been sent to New York to help U Thant in his negotiations to overcome the crisis.[27]

Kennedy answered immediately:

> . . . I think that you and I, with our heavy responsibilities for the maintenance of peace, were aware that developments were approaching a point where events could have become unmanageable. So I welcome this message and consider it an important contribution to peace. The distinguished efforts of Acting Secretary-General U Thant have greatly facilitated both our tasks. I consider my letter to you of October twenty-seventh and your reply of today as firm undertakings on the part of both our governments which should be promptly carried out. I hope that the necessary measures can at once be taken through the United Nations, as your message says, so that the United States in turn will be able to remove the quarantine measures now in effect. I have already made arrangements to report all these matters to the Organization of American States, whose members share a deep interest in a genuine peace in the Caribbean area.

He then explained the recent violation of Soviet territory by an American plane and expressed his regrets. Finally, pointing to the advantages for the two powers in being able to pursue their domestic goals free from the fear of war, he agreed that urgent attention should be directed to the problem of disarmament, suggesting that priority should be given to questions relating to the proliferation of nuclear weapons and to the effort for a nuclear test ban.[28] In a brief statement published the same day, Kennedy welcomed Khrushchev's 'statesmanlike decision' and expressed his hopes for an end to the arms race and a reduction in world tensions.[29]

Though the American government had to give a conditional undertaking not to invade Cuba, the agreement reached by the superpowers clearly represented a victory for the United States. The reasons why the Soviet Union had to accept diplomatic defeat were several. First, the discovery of the missile bases before they were operational allowed the United States to put pressure on the Soviet Union before the latter was in a position to take full advantage of its initiative. Second, American naval superiority in the region made it possible for the United States to use the weapon of 'quarantine', but hard for the Soviet Union to break the blockade. Third, the global strategic superiority of the United States compelled the Soviet government to avoid escalation of the conflict. Probably, the local advantages of the United States were more important than its global superiority in making the Soviet Union back down.

President Kennedy's way of handling the actual confrontation must have made it easier for the Soviet leaders to accept that they were at a disadvantage in the conflict and to draw the appropriate conclusions. 'President Kennedy,' his brother wrote, 'dedicated himself to making it clear to Khrushchev by word and deed—for both are important—that the US had limited objectives and that we had no interest in accomplishing those objectives by adversely affecting the national security of the Soviet Union or by humiliating her'.[30] Certainly, once the Americans had decided to meet the Russian challenge in open confrontation, they showed considerable restraint in their actions and reactions, avoiding as far as possible backing the opponent into a corner. At several crucial stages, they displayed special prudence in refraining from making triumphant noises at signs of success, which might well have made it more difficult for the Russians to retreat.[31]

Negotiating the agreement between the superpowers had been a strictly bilateral business. Carrying it out involved third parties, particularly Castro's Cuba. During the week of confrontation, both of the protagonists had more or less ignored Castro. While Kennedy had separated his immediate issue with the Soviet Union from the long-term conflict with Cuba by deciding only to deal directly with the Soviet government, Khrushchev seems to have simplified his decision-making by not consulting Castro about his moves. The Cuban leader had reacted strongly to being ignored and left in the dark. In a speech delivered on 23 October he had accused Kennedy of piracy and had refused all inspection of Cuba. In addition, he had declared a general mobilisation and, on 26 October, had directed an appeal to China. Other acts had underlined the belligerent and unaccommodating attitude of the Cuban government. The Soviet tanker *Bucharest*, which was allowed through the blockade, had been given a rapturous welcome; and the shooting down of the U-2 plane had been greeted with such triumph as to suggest that it was the achievement of a Cuban crew. A letter from U Thant, in which the Secretary General asked for a suspension of measures likely to aggravate the situation, had been answered only after some delay and then with a brief note rejecting the request and insisting on Cuba's right to possess all the arms it considered necessary.

When the news of the agreement between the superpowers

reached Cuba, Castro became furious. His anger was directed not only at the Americans but also at the Russians, who obviously had omitted to consult him about the terms for ending the confrontation. Feeling betrayed by his ally, he immediately reacted by broadcasting a long statement setting out his own terms for an agreement. These included the end of the economic blockade of Cuba, the end of subversive activities in Cuba, the end of 'pirate attacks' from bases in the United States and Puerto Rico, the end of violations of air and naval space by American aircraft and ships and withdrawal of United States forces from the naval base at Guantanamo.[32] In his resistance to the deal which the Soviet government had arranged with the United States, Castro received the support of China. On 31 October the Chinese, who had supported the Soviet Union publicly during the confrontation, published an article under the title 'The Cry of the People is: Defend the Cuban Revolution!', in which Castro's five conditions were described as 'completely justified' and 'absolutely necessary'.[33] During the following weeks, the Chinese repeatedly reiterated their solidarity with Cuba and their criticism of Soviet 'capitulationism'.

The first known attempt to persuade Castro to accept the superpower agreement was made by U Thant, who, as emissary of forty-five neutral nations, spent two days in Havana arguing with the Cuban leader about the removal of the missiles under international inspection. Castro, complaining that the Russians had treated him as a vassal, stuck to his five conditions and refused all proposals for UN observation or Red Cross verification. A Brazilian mission to Cuba seems to have been equally unsuccessful.

Only after an extended process of double pressure, by the United States on the Soviet Union and by the Soviet Union on Cuba, was the major part of the agreement, though not all of it, carried into effect. While Kennedy had to use both diplomatic and military pressure to compel Khrushchev to carry out his undertakings, Mikoyan had to bring economic and perhaps also other influence to bear on Castro to force him to accept the terms. In both cases, the negotiations between the parties centred on the issues of inspection and verification in Cuba and of removal of the Ilyushin-28 bombers, which had been classified as offensive weapons.

On 1 November the American government reimposed the blockade, which it had lifted during U Thant's visit to Cuba, and resumed aerial surveillance. In a statement issued the following day, Kennedy announced that the bases in Cuba were being dismantled and the missiles being crated. He declared that the completion of this work would be followed closely by the United States, particularly by means of aerial surveillance, until 'an equally satisfactory international means of verification is effected'.[34] But Mikoyan, who subsequently went to Havana to make the Cuban government give way, failed to persuade Castro to allow inspection in Cuba on terms acceptable to the United States. In the end the missiles were inspected at sea. Shipping them as deck cargo made it possible for the Russian captains to show the missiles to American inspection teams on United States vessels which passed alongside the Soviet ships.

On the matter of the removal of the Ilyushin-28s, too, the United States insisted on dealing directly with the Soviet Union. In an exchange of notes between Kennedy and Khrushchev, as well as through other contacts between the two governments, the President put very strong pressure on the Russians, eventually threatening that if the bombers were not promptly removed they would be destroyed on the ground by the United States Air Force.[35] Mikoyan, in turn, pressed Castro very hard to give up the bombers, which the Cuban government, perhaps rightly, regarded as their property. In the bargaining between the two, Mikoyan, who was able to emphasise Cuban dependence on aid from the Soviet bloc, had the upper hand. It is possible he even threatened that the Soviet Union might abandon Cuba altogether. Eventually, on 19 November, Castro gave in and announced his agreement to the withdrawal of the Soviet bombers.

On 20 November Kennedy declared the final ending of the 'quarantine'. His announcement was followed the next day by a Soviet order 'standing down' the forces mobilised during the crisis. For weeks afterwards, Soviet and American delegates were involved in negotiations about withdrawal of Russian military technicians from Cuba. It was not until 7 January 1963 that the two governments finally put an end to the crisis by having their representatives send a joint letter to the Secretary General, informing him that, although it had not been possible to resolve all the problems arising from the crisis, the degree of understanding reached between the parties made it unnecessary for this item to occupy further the attention of the Security Council.[36]

The settlement of the crisis was a defeat not only for Castro's Cuba but also for the Cuban exiles in the United States. Though the American government had backed the exile leaders before the crisis, during the confrontation it had frustrated them by paying little more attention to them than to Castro and his colleagues. The news of the superpower agreement, which reached the exiles just when they were thinking that invasion and liberation of Cuba were imminent, left them deeply disappointed. To them, Kennedy's offer to Khrushchev to give assurances against an invasion of Cuba seemed a betrayal. In the end, of course, Kennedy did not give a public undertaking to refrain from invading Cuba, on the grounds that the removal of the missiles had taken place without the international inspection which was the conditional element in his offer. But it seems likely that he privately assured Khrushchev that it was not his intention to allow an invasion to take place. At any rate, the fifteen years that have passed since that crisis have seen no attempt to invade Cuba from United States territory.

Thus, in effect, the conflict in the Caribbean was settled at the expense of both Cubas. While the Soviet Union deprived the Cuban government of its new weapons, the United States denied the exiles the opportunity to return to their country in force. As far as relations with the Cubans were concerned, the essence of the settlement was an agreement that each superpower would check its Cuban ally. This implicit deal was negotiated over the heads of both parties to the local conflict and carried out in the face of their opposition. Thus intramural relations on both sides of the East-West conflict were sacrificed for the sake of terminating an adversary crisis.

As with the clash in the Taiwan Strait in 1958, the efforts of the United States and the Soviet Union to prevent the crisis from getting out of control may be divided into four kinds. First, both of the powers exercised a great deal of self-restraint in the actual confrontation. By concentrating on immediate interests, they contained the issue; by keeping ideological argument and mutual abuse at a relatively low level, they controlled tension; and by acting and reacting with utmost caution, they prevented violence and escalation of the conflict. The self-control displayed by the Americans in tactics and style, though not in the uncompromising stance they had assumed, was particularly important, since the United States had the upper hand in the region. By choosing the least offensive measures required for their set purpose of making the Russians back down in open confrontation, by carrying them out with firmness, and by giving the opponent good time to think after each move, the American decision-makers helped to encourage prudence on the part of the Soviet leaders and to prevent misunderstandings and overreactions.

Second, each of the superpowers invoked the nuclear deterrent. By threatening, both publicly and in private messages, to retaliate if nuclear weapons were used, the two statesmen compelled each other not to escalate the conflict to the critical level. In the direct confrontation of this crisis, the threat of retaliation was clearly more important as a restraining influence on the superpowers than it was in the Far Eastern crisis.

Third, both of the superpowers checked their Cuban satellites in the later stage of the crisis. Before, as well as at the height of the clash, each backed its ally, the Soviet Union by supplying the weapons to the Cuban government and, during the confrontation, by defending its right to possess whatever armaments it considered necessary for the defence of Cuban territory, the United States by underwriting the exiles' programme of liberating their country and, during the confrontation, by threatening invasion. At the end of the confrontation stage, however, each of the two powers abruptly reversed its policy towards its ally, the Soviet Union withdrawing the weapons and the United States agreeing, privately or tacitly, not to invade Cuba. Since Khrushchev, as the challenger in the crisis, had made more use of Castro's Cuba for his purposes than Kennedy had of the exiles, the reversal of policy was more marked in the Soviet case than in the American.

Fourth, each superpower did what it could do compel the opponent to check its Cuban ally. Just as self-restraint was reinforced in the confrontation by the nuclear threat from the opponent, so in the later stages of the crisis constraint of the ally was backed on each side by pressure from the other superpower. Since the Russo-American agreement itself as well as its implementation resulted largely from this mutual pressure, it was of crucial importance in the termination of the crisis. Compared with the clash over the offshore islands, both the checking of the allies and the mutual pressure of the superpowers to make their curb effective played a much greater role in the settlement of the crisis.

In contrast with their behaviour in the clash over Quemoy and Matsu, the Soviet Union and the United States moved closer to each other during the Cuban missile crisis. In the measures they took to control tension and prevent escalation they reached a certain reciprocity; and in the efforts they made to put their agreement into effect they developed some interaction. But, despite their solidarity of purpose in avoiding nuclear war, the two powers did not at any stage come sufficiently close to each other to develop elements of condominium in their relationship. It was not through joint efforts of the superpowers that either of their Cuban allies was checked. Though Mikoyan apparently went to Cuba with the blessings of the American government, he represented only the Soviet Union in his negotiations with Castro. Throughout the crisis, the United States refused to deal with the Cuban government, exercising its pressure on Castro not jointly *with* the Soviet Union but indirectly, *through* the Soviet Union.

Nor would it be correct to say that the two powers managed the crisis by privately concerting or tacitly coordinating their separate efforts, if concert implies a harmonious relationship and coordination a balanced reciprocity. The settlement came about primarily as a result of the exceedingly strong pressure which the Americans brought to bear on the Soviet government; and the terms of the agreement were considerably more favourable to the United States than to the Soviet Union. Though in retrospect the American agreement not only to lift the blockade but also to refrain from invading Cuba may seem a fairly substantial concession, at the time the Soviet undertaking to remove the missiles and other offensive weapons from Cuban territory was generally regarded as much the more onerous part of the bargain. This evident imbalance both in the terms of the agreement and in the manner of its execution gave rise to a notion of crisis management rather different from that entertained by some of those writers who in recent years have looked to the superpowers for joint action to control and overcome international crises. It led to the idea of *one* superpower managing a crisis by compelling the other one to back down without resort to war.[37]

The rather one-sided character of the management of this crisis was the result of the advantages the United States enjoyed and the way it put them to use. In more than one sense, the Cuban missile crisis was President Kennedy's crisis. Though the original challenge came from the Soviet Union, it was Kennedy and his advisers who decided to settle the issue through an open, physical confrontation. By focusing the attention of the world on the missiles and demanding their removal, Kennedy defined the terms of the crisis. By using America's local superiority in conventional weapons, he compelled Khrushchev and his colleagues to choose between giving in and suffer inevitable humiliation or raising the level of the conflict and perhaps cause a nuclear exchange. Having decided on the form of the confrontation, specified the matter at issue and forced Khrushchev to back down, the American government was in a position to play down its own concessions. Consequently, the settlement came to appear as an even more lop-sided exercise in crisis management than it actually was.

Contrary to the case of the Taiwan Strait crisis, the settlement of the Cuban missile crisis did have some bearing on the underlying issues of the conflict. If, on the one hand, the basic issue had to do with the arms race and the balance of power between the superpowers, the settlement did establish that it was not possible for one of the parties to bring about a sudden change in the global balance by installing missiles in an area traditionally within the sphere of interest of the other power. If, on the other hand, the principal underlying issue concerned relations between the United States and Cuba, the settlement did in fact put a stop to any American plans for invading Cuba and toppling Castro by force.

Though the conduct of the superpowers in this crisis hardly amounted to a precedent in joint crisis management, it did help to initiate a certain détente in East-West relations. The shock of the confrontation as well as the subsequent realisation that luck, despite the skill and nerve displayed by both parties, had played no small part in averting a major war both helped to bring it home to the governments of the two powers that direct confrontations between them had to be avoided in the future. The experience of this clash also convinced the two governments that some machinery ought to be introduced to deal with future East-West crises. After October 1962, statements by Soviet and American leaders about sharing responsibility for preserving the peace of the world and maintaining the order of international society seemed to amount to more than mere rhetoric.

4 Middle East 1967

The last East-West crisis to be examined here occurred in a global political context rather different from that which had obtained in the three earlier situations of conflict. Firstly, growing scientific cooperation and other forms of contact between the superpowers and increased trade and improved diplomatic relations between the two halves of Europe had brought about a gradual decline in Cold War tensions since the confrontation of October 1962. Secondly, the widening rift between China and the Soviet Union on one side and France's assertions of independence of its NATO partners on the other had made the bipolar pattern of international relations less well defined than it had been in the fifties and early-sixties. Thirdly, the military involvement of the United States and the political interest of the Soviet Union and China in the war in Vietnam had already provided a hint of the triangular pattern of international conflict which later on was to emerge on a global scale. But the still high level of tension between the Soviet Union and the United States, the intense absorption of China in domestic affairs and the immense strategic inferiority of this and other secondary powers allowed the dualistic structure to survive more or less unimpaired for some time yet, both in the central balance of power and in some local balances. The Middle Eastern crisis of 1967, far from being an early exercise in triangular rivalry, was a late high-point in the duel of the superpowers.

Unlike the confrontation over Cuba, the clash in the Middle East was not a crisis of the central balance of power. The events of May and June 1967, arising as they did from tension and war between Arab states and Israel, were rooted in the local balance of the Middle East. Though in the event the crisis very nearly led the Soviet Union and the United States into physical confrontation with each other, they were involved as potential interventionists, as principals of the actual protagonists and not as parties to the conflict. Having long encouraged or supported their clients in the region, the superpowers found themselves drawn closer and closer to a local conflict which, were they to intervene, might well develop into a global clash.

The 1967 crisis went through three major phases. The first, the 'upswing phase', which began on 14 May with Nasser mobilising his armed forces and two days later requesting the United Nations to withdraw its peace-keeping force in the Sinai, ended with the outbreak of war on 5 June. The second, the peak of the crisis, lasted from 5 till 10 June, the duration of the Six Day War. The third, the aftermath, began with the cease-fire on the 10th and petered out some time after the meeting between Kosygin and Johnson at Glassboro two weeks later. To determine the nature of the interaction of the superpowers in the crisis, it is necessary to examine their conduct in each of the three phases, particularly their attempts to restrain the parties directly involved in the conflict and their efforts to keep themselves out of the hostilities.

In the upswing phase, a number of interested parties apart from the two superpowers tried to play an intermediary role in the conflict, some channelling their initiatives through the United Nations and others acting outside that arena. None of them was able to exert much influence on the course of events. The United Nations was virtually powerless. The first reaction of this body was to respond to Nasser's request and almost immediately withdraw the United Nations Emergency Force, which since the Suez crisis had acted as a buffer between Egypt and Israel. Subsequently, the Secretary General flew to Cairo to confer with Nasser, returning to the United Nations headquarters on 25 May to report that the situation in the Near East was 'more disturbing, indeed . . . more menacing than at any time since the fall of 1956'.[1] Between 24 and 31 May, the Security Council, convened at the request of Canada and Denmark, held five meetings to consider the situation. The Council had before it three draft resolutions, submitted by Canada and Denmark, by the United States and by the United Arab Republic; but disagreement between the United States and the Soviet Union prevented it from reaching a decision and taking action. Throughout this phase the Security Council was in effect paralysed.

The two most important initiatives taken by non-superpowers outside the United Nations were those of France and Britain. On 24 May the French government, which till then had been silent about the crisis, proposed that the four great powers—the United States, the Soviet Union, Britain and France—should concert their efforts in the interests of peace. This proposal, which amounted to a revival of the post-war idea of a concert of the Big Four, was backed by the argument that the Security Council would be able to agree on concrete measures only if the four powers had reached agreement among themselves.[2] But the French plan, too, foundered on disagreement between the superpowers. While the representative of the United States announced in the Security Council that his government was prepared to join with the other three great powers in a common effort to restore and maintain peace in the Middle East, the Soviet Union turned down President de Gaulle's suggestion. France reacted at first by taking up a position of strict neutrality in the dispute and later by adopting an anti-Israeli policy.

The policy of the British, on the other hand, at this stage of the crisis, was to cooperate with the Americans. They proposed two steps. First, they suggested a public declaration, signed by as many countries as possible, reasserting the right of free passage through the Gulf of Aqaba, which the Egyptians had closed to Israeli shipping. Second, they wanted to set up a naval task force, made up of detachments from as many nations as possible, to break Nasser's blockade and open the Strait of Tiran. The United States accepted the British plan, and the two governments set out to solicit the support and participation of other nations. Their efforts, however, drew only a very meagre response. This, together with a certain hesitation in Washington and London, which probably arose from fear of the possible effects of a physical intervention in the dispute, guaranteed that no multilateral action was taken in time to prevent an outbreak of war.

The failure of the French and British initiatives demonstrated unequivocally that de Gaulle's idea of four more or less equal great powers was an illusion. After its unsuccessful attempt to set up a concert of the world, France found it expedient to move to a marginal position in the conflict. Britain, who it is alleged had first considered and rejected a plan to intervene on its own,[3] found itself unable to act effectively even in association with the United States. The secondary powers had to leave any further attempt to control the course of the developing crisis to the two superpowers.

Since the Arab states held the initiative in this phase of the crisis, the Soviet Union, their principal, had a more important role than the United States. Though our knowledge of Soviet policy is far less detailed than that of American, the general character of the Soviet government's attitude to the developments in the Middle East seems fairly clear. A certain degree of ambiguity seems to have characterised the Russian line. While at the outset of the crisis the Soviet Union probably encouraged Egypt to take threatening measures against Israel, in the next stages, when war was approaching, it made some attempts to restrain its client.

The Soviet Government played an important part even in the initiation of the crisis. It was from Soviet sources that Nasser's government received the dubious news of an Israeli plan for a large-scale attack on Syria.[4] By passing on to the Egyptians what may have been merely an Israeli contingency plan and thus encouraging Nasser to move his troops into Sinai, the Russians presumably sought to demonstrate their loyalty to the Syrians, with whom they lately had become deeply involved. In the following weeks, too, the Soviet Union went out of its way to emphasise its support of Syria and Egypt. On 23 May the government issued a formal statement in which it reviewed the origins of the crisis and warned that 'should anyone try to unleash aggression in the Near East, he would be met not only with the united strength of Arab countries but also with strong opposition to aggression from the Soviet Union and all peace-loving countries'.[5] Some days later Kosygin must have reassured the Egyptian Defence Minister that the Soviet Union would neutralise the United States in the event of war in the Middle East. At any rate, Nasser, in a speech to the National Assembly on 29 May, was able to report that he had received a message from the Soviet Premier which said that 'the Soviet Union stands with us in this battle and will never allow any state to intervene until things go back to what they were in 1956'.[6] Two days later the Russians were reported to be moving additional naval units to the eastern Mediterranean. And, of course, during this period the Soviet Union was also supporting the Arab states in the United Nations.

But, though the Soviet government supplied the initial en-couragement to Egypt and subsequently supported the Arab states in public, there are good reasons to believe that it became increasingly concerned about the possible consequences of the actions taken by Nasser. While the Soviet leaders may well have wanted the Egyptians to move into Sinai, it is doubtful whether they were consulted about the request for withdrawal of UNEF, and fairly certain that they were startled by the proclamation of the blockade. With the likelihood of a strong reaction from Israel and its friends, the Russians must have feared not only a defeat of Egypt, about whose state of preparedness they were better informed than most, but also a confrontation with the United States. This would explain why, when the Americans told the Russians that they had received information from Israel indicating that Egypt might be planning to attack on 27 May, the Soviet government had its ambassador in Cairo call Nasser out of bed at 3.30 in the morning with an earnest warning to exercise restraint. (About the same time it sent a note to the Israeli Prime Minister, urging his government to take all possible measures to prevent a military conflict.) Descriptions of the Soviet attitude between then and the outbreak of war vary from mild concern to alarm. It does seem that Moscow, unhappy about the call for a 'holy war', addressed several words of warning to Arab leaders before 5 June.[7]

The contrast between encouragement and restraint in the Soviet attitude to the Arab states might be seen as the result of disagreement among the Russian leaders. There may have been a clash between 'hawks', some of whom may even have favoured a war by proxy in the Middle East, and 'doves', who may have been determined to avoid any local conflict which could lead to a global confrontation. If this was the situation in Moscow, it seems that the former group had the upper hand in the initial stage of the crisis, but that the latter gained influence as war was seen to become imminent. Another possible explanation for Soviet ambiguity is miscalculation. Perhaps the government, thinking that it would be able to strengthen its influence in the Middle East by inciting the Arab states to step up pressure on Israel, calculated that the ensuing tension would not lead to war. If so, the Soviet leaders may have decided to try to draw back when it became clear that events were in danger of getting out of control. A third possibility is that the Soviet government at first simply overreacted to Israeli moves.

Whether it arose from indecision, miscalculation or some other source, Soviet policy in the up-swing phase was hardly successful. If the Soviet government, for whatever reasons, attempted to manipulate the Egyptians at the outset of the crisis, this gave Nasser an opportunity to escalate the conflict and draw the principal closer to his side. The result was that the Russians, instead of using the Egyptians for their own ends, ended up being used by the Egyptians for *their* purposes. Though the Soviet government in the last week or two before the outbreak of war may have warned the Arabs to exercise restraint, it was unable to control the course of events effectively by influencing the conduct of its clients. The Soviet

Union could not be said to have managed the up-swing phase of the crisis—except, perhaps, in the sense of having initiated the clash.

For the United States, principal of the state that was threatened and challenged by Nasser's moves, there were two ways of attempting to influence the reactions of its client in order to avert war. One was to temper and check the Arab states, the other to reassure and restrain Israel. The United States tried both. In addition to the various unsuccessful attempts at multilateral action already mentioned—through the Security Council of the United Nations, through a concert of the Big Four, and by means of an international naval task force—the Americans made some efforts to influence the Arab governments directly. On 22 May, shortly before the announcement by Egypt that it was closing the Gulf of Aqaba to Israeli shipping, President Johnson sent a letter to Nasser. Assuring him of America's basic friendship for Egypt, Johnson urged the Egyptian leader to avoid war as his paramount duty and expressed the hope that, 'if we come through these days without hostilities', he could send Vice President Humphrey to talk to him and other leaders in the Middle East in a new attempt to solve the old problems of that region.[8] Four days later Johnson sent a note to the Egyptian ambassador in Washington, requesting the Egyptians to use restraint and not to open fire first.[9] On the last day of the month, a former American Secretary of the Treasury spoke to Nasser and arranged for the Vice President of the United Arab Republic to come to Washington on 7 June for personal discussions.[10] The outbreak of war prevented this visit.

But the main thrust of American diplomacy in this period was directed at Israel. At the outset of the crisis, the United States was afraid that Israeli anxiety about withdrawal of UNEF might lead to hasty action and open conflict. Thus, on 17 May Johnson sent a cable to the Israeli Prime Minister spelling out his deep concern and urging restraint. 'I am sure you will understand', he wrote, 'that I cannot accept any responsibilities on behalf of the United States for situations which arise as the result of actions on which we are not consulted.'[11] Nasser's decision to close the Gulf of Aqaba aggravated the situation and involved the United States more deeply on the side of Israel. Recognising that right of access to the Gulf was part of the commitment the United States had given to Israel in 1957, the President broadcast a statement on 23 May with the aim of giving some assurance to the Israelis. The United States, he declared, 'considers the Gulf to be an international waterway and feels that a blockade of Israeli shipping is illegal and potentially disastrous to the cause of peace'. He also reaffirmed the American commitment to support the political independence and territorial integrity of all the nations of the area.[12]

Three days later Johnson had a 'direct and frank' conversation with Israel's Foreign Minister, who had flown to Washington for consultations. With obvious concern Eban related that, according to Israeli intelligence reports, the United Arab Republic was preparing an all-out attack. The President replied that American intelligence indicated that an attack was not imminent, adding that, if the Arabs did attack, Israel would 'whip hell out of them'. In answer to a question about what the United States was willing to do to keep the Gulf open, Johnson assured Eban that the Americans were hard at work planning what to do to ensure free passage, and when to do it. They first had to try to work through the United Nations, he pointed out. If that body proved ineffective, the time would have come for Israel and her friends to give specific indication of what they could do. Johnson said he saw some hope in the British plan for an international naval force in the Strait area but emphasised the need to have the support of Congress. Israel, he urged, should concentrate its efforts on the task of winning support for this plan from other governments. 'The central point, Mr. Minister', the President said, according to his own account of the conversation, 'is that your nation not be the one to bear the responsibility for any outbreak of war.' Israel, he stressed, 'will not be alone unless it decides to go alone'.[13] Shortly after this meeting the American ambassador to Israel delivered a note to Eshkol, making much the same points.[14]

Soon after receiving these various assurances and calls for restraint from the United States, Israel decided to postpone military action. As a result, a certain relaxation seems to have developed in Washington. Since they had heard from Eshkol that Israel would give them another week or two to bring the international naval escort into play, the Americans continued the search for a multilateral solution but with less urgency. Less than a week later Israel went into action. Johnson's account of the crisis shows just how disappointed the American government was at their failure to forestall war.

The action-reaction relationship of the four parties most immediately involved in this phase of the crisis was a complex one. Since the United States' incentive to intervene arose largely from concern about the danger of precipitous Israeli action, the determination of the American government to act declined markedly when the Israeli government appeared nervous about the possibility of an Arab attack and hesitant about the idea of acting on its own. Since the Soviet Union's inhibitions about encouraging the Arab states sprang no doubt largely from concern about the intentions of the United States, the indecision of the American government must have tended to weaken Soviet efforts to restrain the Arabs. At the same time, the tame reactions and hesitant attitude of the United States encouraged Egypt to proceed with its challenge to Israel. Finally, the pressure of the Arab states together with the ineffectiveness of American diplomacy pushed the Israelis towards acting on their own. Thus, the superpowers not only failed to restrain their clients but, by reacting too weakly to the unfolding situation, in effect actually encouraged them to move towards war.

Though the superpowers were unable to prevent the clash, they did manage to achieve a limited degree of diplomatic cooperation in their relations with the protagonists and to come to some understanding about their own reactions to events in the up-swing phase of the crisis. Washington and Moscow were in touch with each other about the situation not only through their embassies and through their representatives at the United Nations but also, from 22 May, at the highest level. On that day the President sent Kosygin a message appealing for cooperation in the efforts to calm the situation. Johnson quotes the following passage in his account of the crisis:

> The increasing harassment of Israel by elements based in Syria with attendant reactions within Israel and within the Arab world, has brought the area close to major violence. Your and our ties to nations of the area could bring us into difficulties which I am confident neither of us seeks. It would appear a time for each of us to use our influence to the full in the cause of moderation, including our influence over action by the United Nations.[15]

Though neither this nor any of the other exchanges between the two capitals produced any agreement of a constructive kind, they did lead to some concerting of diplomatic efforts in one instance at least. On 25 and 26 May both of the powers arranged for their representatives to deliver notes to Egypt as well as to Israel urging self-restraint. The background to this exercise in parallel diplomacy was Johnson's conversations with Eban in Washington, as a result of which the President informed Moscow of Israel's fear of an Egyptian attack and requested the Soviet government to follow him in cautioning Nasser. The Soviet government apparently agreed on the condition that similar notes were sent to Israel.[16] However, the fact that the Israeli fears were exaggerated reduced the importance of this essay in concerted superpower diplomacy.

A much more important outcome of the exchanges between Washington and Moscow was what seems to have amounted to a mutual understanding that the superpowers would refrain from intervening militarily in the conflict. Since neither the United States nor the Soviet Union considered the interests involved worth a world war, their supreme concern at this stage of the crisis must have been to avoid a direct confrontation and head-on collision between themselves. Through formal and informal contacts each apparently managed to communicate to the other that it did not intend to intervene directly provided the other one took the same line.[17] This understanding was bolstered, not undermined, by the declarations of support of the clients and the verbal warnings to the other side issued by each of the superpowers, and even more so by the naval movements ordered by each.

Though this agreement of the superpowers helped to prevent world war, it made a local war more likely. As already suggested, the knowledge that the Americans had no intention of becoming involved and that the Russians could neutralise them in the event of war made it seem less risky for Egypt to persevere with its challenge to Israel and more necessary for Israel to respond with force. Also, the belief of the superpowers that, if war did break out, it could be limited to the region made it more tempting for the Russian government to encourage the Egyptians and less imperative for both the Russians and the Americans to restrain their clients. Managing the crisis by localising the conflict did not go hand in hand with controlling the crisis by restraining the parties.

When the up-swing phase of the crisis gave way to open hostilities, these two approaches to crisis management became more compatible. Since, with the outbreak of war, the danger of the Soviet Union and the United States being drawn into hostilities on opposite sides became more immediate, the need to restrain the parties and put an end to hostilities became more urgent. Part of the efforts of the superpowers to bring about a cease-fire was channelled

through the United Nations. The Security Council met in emergency session on 5 June after the outbreak of fighting and continued
considering the Middle East situation until the 14th. At the outset of
the debate, the United States and Britain advocated an immediate
cease-fire without conditions, while the Soviet Union and others
held out for a motion which condemned Israel as the aggressor and
demanded a withdrawal to the original positions. But on the 6th,
when the extent of Israeli victories after 36 hours of fighting had
become known, the Soviet Union changed position and gave its
support to a simple call for cease-fire. On that day the Security
Council unanimously passed a resolution which called on the
governments concerned 'as a first step to take forthwith all measures
for an immediate cease-fire and for a cessation of all military
activities in the area'.[18] Immediately, an appeal to stop the fighting
went to Israel and the Arab states; and early on 7 June Israel
announced that it was willing to accept a cease-fire, on the condition
that the Arabs agreed. But some of the Arabs went on fighting,
Jordan alone accepting a cease-fire on that day. Though an
agreement was reached with the United Arab Republic on the
following day, an effective cease-fire was not worked out with Syria
till 10 June.

In the meantime, however, the two superpowers had tabled
competing draft resolutions. On 8 June the United States had
submitted one which called both for a cease-fire and for longer-
range discussions, while the Soviet Union on the same day had
introduced another which condemned Israel's 'aggressive activities'
and its 'violations' of the earlier cease-fire resolutions. Thus began
the great issue of the post-war years about a Middle Eastern peace
settlement and Israeli withdrawal of occupation forces.

The Security Council was too divided for its members to bring
concerted pressure to bear on the parties. But separately, the
superpowers seem to have exerted some influence on both sides. On
the first day of the war, the Soviet Union and the United States,
equally concerned about the danger of the war escalating to a level
where they might become involved, appear to have taken very
nearly parallel courses, particularly in relation to Egypt. Though
little information is available about what passed between the Soviet
government and the Arab leaders on that day, we know that the
Soviet ambassador to the United Nations suggested to his American
counterpart that the latter see the representative of the United Arab
Republic, and that Goldberg subsequently urged upon Egypt the

need to move quickly towards a settlement and a mutual withdrawal from the Sinai.[19] It is reasonable to assume that the
Russians, too, cautioned the Egyptians at this stage.

On the following days, however, the two powers took very
different lines in their relations with the belligerent states. Since it
was Israel, the country that had initiated open hostilities, which was
winning the war, the role of exercising restraint from outside fell
primarily to the United States. This function it seems to have
performed towards the end rather than in the earliest days of the
war. If at first the Americans were guilty of stalling for time to allow
Israel to complete its military operations, on the last day or two of
the war they used, as Johnson put it, 'every diplomatic resource' to
make Israel come to an effective cease-fire with Syria.[20] The Soviet
Union, backing the loser, was exposed to other pressures and took a
different course. With the Arabs rapidly approaching a disastrous
defeat and urgently clamouring for assistance, the Soviet government swung towards a policy of strong diplomatic and political
support for its clients, particularly Syria, and opposition to Israel
and its friends. As a result, the superpowers ended up in sharp
opposition to each other.

At the end of the war, the United States and the Soviet Union
even found themselves on the threshold of military confrontation.
Johnson relates how, on the morning of the tenth, when reports
indicated that a cease-fire with Syria was being arranged, he was
called to the hot-line equipment to receive from Kosygin what
turned out to be the most threatening message of the whole crisis.
The Soviet government accused Israel of ignoring all Security
Council resolutions for a cease-fire. 'Kosygin,' the President reports,
'said a "very crucial moment" had now arrived. He spoke of the
possibility of "independent decision" by Moscow. He foresaw the
risk of a "grave catastrophe" and stated that unless Israel
unconditionally halted operations within the next few hours, the
Soviet Union would take "necessary actions, including military".'[21]
Johnson's immediate reaction was to enquire about the position of
the Sixth Fleet. Knowing that Soviet intelligence ships were
monitoring the fleet's every movement, he told McNamara to issue
orders at once to change the course of the fleet and cut the limitation
on the minimum distance of the ships from the Syrian coast from one
hundred to fifty miles. Thus he made it clear to the Soviet leaders
that the United States was prepared to resist Soviet military action
in the Middle East. Soon after this move Johnson sent a reply to

Kosygin on the hot line. In what he describes as a 'temperate and factual' message, the President told Kosygin that he believed the United Nations negotiator to be very close to completing a cease-fire agreement between Israel and Syria, that the United States had been pressing Israel to make this cease-fire completely effective and that he had received assurances this would be done. Throughout that morning there were further exchanges on the hot line. As Israel and Syria moved to a cease-fire, Kosygin's messages grew more temperate. Eventually Johnson could close the exchange with the usual expression of hope that the future efforts of the two powers would be devoted to achieving lasting peace throughout the world.[22]

In the course of the six days of hostilities the Soviet Union and the United States, in their dealings with their clients in the Middle East, moved from a relationship verging on cooperation to one of hostile rivalry. The first exchange on the hot line, on the morning of the fifth, contained a hint of concerted efforts to influence the warring parties. Kosygin said that the Russians intended to work for a cease-fire and hoped the Americans would exert influence on Israel, and Johnson answered that the Americans would use all their influence to halt hostilities and were pleased the Russians planned to do the same.[23] It is also reported that the Americans, in their first formal policy meeting at this stage of the crisis, discussed the possibility of working with the Soviet Union to bring about a cease-fire.[24] And Goldberg's meeting with the Egyptian representative at the United Nations, since it was arranged at the request of the Soviet ambassador, may be seen not only as an example of parallel action but also as a manifestation of the tendency actually to cooperate on the first day of the war. If, however, the outbreak of war tended to bring the superpowers together, the course it took soon divided them once more. The Soviet Union, seeing the Middle Eastern balance of power moving rapidly against itself, found it necessary to support its clients, eventually to the point of threatening to intervene in the hostilities. The United States, gratified by the performance of its protégé but afraid that the war might escalate and slip out of control, finally found it advisable to check its client and force a cease-fire. While the former moved from privately cautioning to openly and strongly supporting the loser, the latter veered from tacitly supporting to privately but firmly curbing the victor.

Both the Soviet Union and the United States may be said in the end to have acted so as to maintain the balance of power in the local struggle, the one supporting the weaker and the other restraining the stronger side. But in doing so they neither acted according to a concerted plan nor engaged in a tacit coordination of separate efforts. While the war was on, both of them concentrated so much on maintaining or strengthening their own positions in the region that these competing concerns virtually eclipsed their common interests in halting the hostilities and damping down the conflict. They proved as unable to coordinate their efforts to control the course of events in the immediate situation as they were to join in the search for a long-term settlement of the issue between Israel and the Arab states.

On the most important point, however, the Soviet Union and the United States remained in agreement after 5 June: both accepted the need for each of them to keep out of the hostilities. Of course, the temptation to become involved was not very great in either case. While Israeli victories made it unnecessary for the United States to intervene to save its client, a relative lack of strategic mobility made it difficult for the Soviet Union to come to the aid of the losing Arab states. But non-intervention in the war was also the result of deliberate effort. Each of the powers took care to avoid becoming involved itself and did what it could to make sure that its opposite number stayed out too. This relationship of mutual restraint was established as soon as the war started and maintained until the end.

The immediate reaction of both the American and the Soviet leaders to the outbreak of war was to get in touch with each other. While Johnson sent a message to Gromyko expressing dismay and surprise at the news, Kosygin opened the hot line. According to reports, the Soviet leader wanted the President to know that Russia was against war in the Middle East and would not intervene if the United States acted similarly.[25] This might be interpreted as a suggestion for an informal pact of non-intervention. If the initiative for such an agreement came from the Soviet Union, the task of maintaining it, by supporting the opponent in its resolve not to become involved, fell mainly to the United States, which had less incentive to intervene.

At several critical junctures of the war the Americans took steps to prevent misunderstandings which might have led to Soviet intervention, superpower confrontation and general war. Thus, in the hot-line exchange on the sixth, Johnson went out of his way to mention the false Arab allegation that the US carrier-based planes had taken part in attacks on Egypt and to express the hope that Kosygin would emphasise the facts to Cairo. The Kremlin is said to have shown anger at the Egyptian allegation of collusion between Israel, Britain and the United States, which it recognised as an attempt to draw the Soviet Union into the war.[26] On the 8th, Johnson sent Kosygin another message aimed at avoiding dangerous confusion. Over the hot line he explained the incident of the erroneous Israeli attack on the US ship *Liberty* and advised Kosygin that carrier aircraft were on their way to investigate, emphasising that this was the sole purpose of these movements and asking that the proper parties be informed accordingly. Kosygin replied that the information had been relayed immediately to the Egyptians.[27] Finally, on 10 June, as we have seen, the President found it necessary to issue orders for naval movements to deter the Soviet government from carrying out its threats of military action in support of Syria. Whether the Americans explained and appealed over the hot line or whether they threatened by way of physical measures, the Russians did respond, with the result that the informal superpower under- standing not to intervene, apparently already reached, tacitly or otherwise, in the up-swing phase of the crisis, was observed throughout the crucial peak of the conflict.

It is reasonable to conclude that at this stage of the crisis the governments of the two powers succeeded not only in honouring the informal rule proscribing direct hostilities between superpowers, which could be traced back to the aftermath of the Cuban missile crisis, but also in developing a degree of what one writer has called 'tacit coordination' of their efforts to avoid unilateral physical intervention.[28] Yet, as an essay in dual crisis management, of the type limited to localising a conflict simply by staying out of the hostilities, this interaction of the superpowers had some of the lopsided quality characterisitic of their handling of the crisis of October 1962. As in the earlier situation, the United States had the upper hand, mainly because its client was winning the war but also because it enjoyed some strategic superiority in the region. As a result, the American government was able to induce the Russian leadership to exercise self-restraint at crucial junctures of the crisis and even to force it to back down when the two powers were on the threshold of confrontation. In this connection it is significant that Johnson's account of his handling of the crisis has echoes of October 1962. On the seventh, he writes, when it was felt in Washington that Nasser had incurred a stunning loss and that the Russians, after badly miscalculating the ability and strength of the Arabs, had suffered a blow to their prestige, he told the National Security Council that 'one thing we must do now is to develop as few heroes and as few heels as we can'.[29] Three days later, when Kosygin sent his threatening message, Johnson again reacted in Kennedy style, combining tough physical measures with temperate verbal messages. However, the means of communication had improved since 1962. While Kennedy had been forced to communicate with Khrushchev mainly through private correspondence and public statements, Johnson was able to conduct his exchange with Kosygin over the hot line.[30]

The tendency for the rivalry of the superpowers to eclipse their common interests was continued in the aftermath of the crisis. Since neither the Soviet Union nor the United States wanted another war in the Middle East, both had some interest in encouraging the Arab states and Israel to reduce tension in the region and in trying to guide them towards a settlement of their differences. But, though in the first weeks after the cease-fire they did take a number of steps in that direction, in general both governments concentrated on pursuing the interests that divided them. Backing their Middle Eastern clients against each other, the superpowers not only failed to concert or coordinate their various attempts to lead the parties towards an agreement but even helped to bring about the rigidity and tension that were to stand in the way of negotiation and settlement for years to come.

Soon after the war, the Soviet Union set out to build up the Arab states with a view to making them strong enough to resist the pressure of Israel and maintain the Soviet position in the Middle East. Podgorny and Nasser, meeting in Cairo between 21 and 25 June, worked out the details of a deal between their two countries. According to reports, the Russians agreed to help Nasser provided he purged his armed forces of incompetent and corrupt elements.[31] They were willing to assist in the rebuilding of the Egyptian forces but not to support any offensive military initiative. As long as Egypt renounced the idea of settling the conflict by force, it could rely on Soviet support in any attempt to recover the lost territories by diplomatic means. Soviet rearmament of Syria, too, seems to have been conditional upon an undertaking not to resort to force again.[32] Considering the outcome of the Six Day War, it is understandable that the Soviet Union should have wished to rearm its friends as well as to restrain them from going to war again.

At the United Nations, the Soviet Union worked for a resolution calling for unconditional Israeli withdrawal. Kosygin, with a large delegation, appeared in New York and addressed the General Assembly, a move which, in part at least, must have been aimed at boosting Arab morale and increasing Soviet prestige in the Middle East. The principle behind the policy of giving diplomatic support and supplying arms but restricting their use seems to have been to restore the East-West power balance in the Middle East without risking a local war, for this could have resulted in another defeat of the Arabs and perhaps a confrontation with the United States.

While the Soviet Union pursued a policy which could conceivably lead to a negotiated settlement some time in the future, the United States at this time mildly encouraged both parties to come to an early agreement. A settlement of the conflict might allow the Americans, who had important interests in the Middle East, to repair their relationship with the Arabs while remaining on good terms with the Israelis. The immediate post-war period, when the Israeli victories made it possible for the United States and its protégé to put some pressure on the Arabs, seemed a good time to call for negotiations. On 19 June President Johnson, listing his Five Great Principles of Peace in the Middle East, asked rhetorically who it was who would make this peace where all others had failed for twenty years or more. 'Clearly the parties to the conflict,' he answered, 'must be the parties to the peace. Sooner or later it is they . . . who must make a settlement in the area. It is hard to see how it is possible for nations to live together in peace if they cannot learn to reason together.'[33]

But, while publicly calling on both parties to show reason and move towards negotiation, the United States obviously supported Israel against the Arab states. In his speech of the 19th, in the passage preceding that just quoted, the President served notice that he would not press the Israelis to pull back their victorious armies from occupied territory until the Arab nations joined Israel in efforts to promote a peaceful settlement. In the following period the United States, by supporting Israel in the United Nations and elsewhere and, eventually, by resuming arms shipments, came close to identifying with Israel. Just as during the war the American government had called for a cease-fire while supporting the Israelis diplomatically until they had completed their military operations, so after the war it called for a peace while at the same time helping

Israel to preserve the fruits of its victory. As with the Soviet Union, the interest of the United States in promoting a settlement of the conflict was subordinated to its concern about maintaining its position in the rivalry with the other superpower.

Since both the Soviet Union and the United States put the interests that divided them, in the Middle East and elsewhere, above those they shared, they were unable to engage together in a sustained effort to reduce tension and bring the conflict a little closer to settlement. The few attempts they made failed utterly. Gromyko's efforts at working out some formula of agreement with Goldberg at the United Nations were foiled by an Arab protest to the Russians. The summit meeting at Glassboro failed by an even greater margin to lead to a concerting of efforts. More than six months after the meeting, Kosygin came close to claiming that he actually had reached an agreement with Johnson, only to find that the Americans had then changed their views in favour of unreserved support for Israeli expansionism;[34] but it seems clear from Johnson's account of the discussions that there was little common ground between the two leaders. The meetings, which were arranged on Kosygin's initiative after some initial reluctance on Johnson's part, took place on 23 and 25 June. They were hampered by a difference of priorities as well as by basic disagreement on the subject at issue. Johnson, whose primary concern at that time was to start strategic arms talks, complains that whenever he brought up the subject of ABMs and ICBMs, Kosygin changed the subject to the Middle East. 'Each time I mentioned missiles, Kosygin talked about Arabs and Israelis.' And when they did talk about the matter which was Kosygin's main interest, considerable tension developed between them:

> At only one point in our first session did Kosygin seem close to becoming really heated. He said we had talked about territorial integrity before the Middle East war, but we had ended by protecting aggression. He insisted that Israeli troops go back to the original armistice lines, and that the question of opening the Gulf of Aqaba be referred to the International Court of Justice. Then, he said, and the implication was 'only then', could we discuss other problems. At that point, he came close to issuing a threat. Unless we agreed to his formula, he declared, there would be a war—'a very great war'. He said the Arabs would fight with arms if they had them and, if not, with bare hands.

'All troops must be withdrawn at once,' he said. If they fight with weapons, I replied, we would know where they got them. Then I leaned forward and said slowly and quietly: 'Let us understand one another. I hope there will be no war. If there is a war, I hope it will not be a big war. If they fight, I hope they fight with fists and not with guns.' I told him that I hoped both our countries could keep out of any Middle East explosion because 'if we do get into it, it will be a most serious matter'.[35]

After Glassboro the two powers were even further apart on the Middle Eastern issue than they had been before.

Though the Soviet Union took certain steps to prevent its protégés from preparing another war and the United States made some moves to encourage the parties to seek a settlement, the superpowers were unable to coordinate their separate efforts even in a tacit manner. When they both tried, through usual diplomatic channels, at the United Nations or at the summit meeting, to find a way of dealing with the situation left by the war, they failed to reach any basic agreement for a concerted attempt to bring the Arabs and Israelis closer to each other in search of a peace. What is more, they made no progress whatever towards settling the underlying issue of the conflict. As in the earlier stages of the crisis, the Middle East was a field of suspicion and rivalry between the superpowers rather than an area of agreement and cooperation.

In each of the three major phases of the crisis, both the Soviet Union and the United States took some steps to moderate the conduct of the protagonists in the conflict. Sometimes by private warnings or assurances and sometimes by public appeals, they attempted to restrain the parties in order, first, to stave off war, then to terminate it, and finally, to prevent its recurrence. Each of them directed its efforts mainly at its own protégés but occasionally also at the opposite side. In private as well as in public, the two powers often appealed to each other to try harder to exercise control over the clients; and on one occasion, that of the cease-fire negotiations between Syria and Israel on 10 June, the Soviet Union even put pressure on the United States by threatening to take military measures. At a few crucial junctures of the crisis, particularly on the first day of the war, the superpowers actually made some half-hearted attempts to cooperate in curbing the opponents. But they neither managed to concert their measures nor succeeded in developing a tacit coordination of efforts. At best, they engaged in parallel action. On the whole, their attempts to exercise a restraining influence were conspicuously unsuccessful. The superpowers exerted less control over the local parties in this conflict than in any of the other three international crises examined here.

In one respect, however, the superpowers were successful. They managed to keep themselves and each other out of the hostilities. And in their endeavour to avoid unilateral intervention they did develop a degree of cooperation in encouraging and restraining each other, even though the influence of the United States over the Soviet Union in this respect was much greater than *vice versa*. Clearly, they found it much easier to cooperate in pursuit of the negative aim of avoiding a major war than in attempts to achieve the more positive goals of moderating the conflict and influencing the parties in the direction of a negotiated settlement.

The fact that the Soviet Union and the United States were far less successful in managing the crisis than in limiting the conflict had to do with their whole conception of this clash in the Middle East. They seemed to see it not so much as a calamity which called for joint action as an opportunity or a challenge which required each of them to act in pursuit or defence of its own interests. Because each of them hoped to strengthen or protect its position in the global issue by backing one side in the local conflict, they engaged in a rivalry by proxy. Consequently the superpowers, in spite of their various efforts to moderate the clash, on the whole helped to exacerbate tension. This held true in each of the three phases of the crisis. While, at the earliest stage, the Soviet Union played a part in initiating the crisis and, during the war, the United States delayed its attempts to put an end to hostilities, after the war both acted in such a way as to maintain rather than to reduce tension. Since the limiting consideration was the risk of major war, the tentative agreement of the superpowers to avoid intervention and prevent escalation helped to remove their inhibitions in engaging in the indirect form of rivalry. The result was that the hostile competition of the two powers all but eclipsed their would-be role of joint crisis managers.

However, the reasons for this outcome was not only that the Soviet Union and the United States, whilst recognising the paramount need to avoid a major war, put their separate and conflicting concerns above their common interests, but also that in each phase of the crisis they became increasingly dependent on their clients. They could not use the local powers in the global rivalry without being used by them for their ends. While the Arabs drew the Soviet Union towards military intervention against Israel, the Israelis manoeuvred the United States into a position close to diplomatic opposition to the Arab states. This, of course, accentuated the conflict between the superpowers, making it even more difficult for them to act together to control the course of events in the Middle East.

Similarly, the self-seeking policies of the superpowers and their dependence on their protégés made it both less expedient and more difficult for them to tackle the underlying issue of the conflict. Their record in this respect contrasts with that of the Cuban missile crisis. The conflict of 1962, since it had led to an open and direct confrontation between the superpowers, had to be settled somehow. But that of 1967, which—despite the incident on 10 June—remained essentially only an indirect East-West clash, could more safely be left as an open issue. While in the former crisis the risk of nuclear war had compelled the superpowers to move beyond challenge and response towards agreement, in the latter situation the agreement to avoid major war allowed them to continue their rivalry in the region. However, even if the Soviet Union and the United States had been both willing and able to reach a Middle-Eastern concord, they would have found it much more difficult to impose their terms on the local parties than it had been in 1962. The determination of the Arabs and the Israelis to continue their struggle left little hope of achieving a lasting settlement after the Six Day War.

5 Restrained Conflict

In the Western language of international politics, the term 'crisis management', which gained currency in the 1960s, originally referred to the art of winning diplomatic victory. For policy-makers as well as for writers, managing an international crisis generally meant making the opponent of the United States and its allies back down without resort to war. When Mr McNamara, in the aftermath of the Cuban missile crisis, remarked that 'there is no longer any such thing as strategy, only crisis management', he was prescribing for the conduct of the United States' relations with the Communist powers. Those American writers who devoted attention to the subject in the following years tended to discuss crisis management in terms of national policy-making. And those non-American Westerners who, in the same period, explored the possibility of securing for the allies of the United States a larger part in the handling of East-West crises clearly operated with an equally one-sided notion of crisis management.[1]

In more recent writings, 'crisis management' has often been used rather differently. It has come to stand for a process in which both of the superpowers take steps to control the course of an international crisis in order to prevent the outbreak of a major war. This notion is related to one which emerged at about the same time as the earlier conception of crisis management. Indeed, the current idea of crisis management may be seen as marking a fall-back position for that of 'condominium'. The latter term—or its various synonyms 'co-imperium', 'diarchy', 'duopoly' etc.—was used by many writers in the West and elsewhere who, in the period following the East-West détente, speculated about the future relationship and role of the United States and the Soviet Union. It generally referred to a degree of superpower control of the international political process bordering on joint government of the world or a large part of it. 'Crisis management', in the present sense of the term, signifies a rather less ambitious programme for the superpowers. It casts them for the parts of backstoppers, of providers of an emergency service.

The idea of a Russo-American condominium came up at a time when the United States still enjoyed considerable strategic superiority over the Soviet Union. In the projected arrangement of world politics, the United States naturally often appeared as the senior and the Soviet Union as the junior partner. While some of those who entertained the notion of condominium spelt out clearly the inequality of roles, others did not.[2] But even those who did not may have taken comfort from the assumption that the Russians would not be able to secure the upper hand in the exercise of joint control. In the late sixties, when the Soviet Union was moving towards equality of strategic power with the United States, the establishment of condominium came to seem not only less possible but also, from a Western point of view, rather less desirable. In the new situation of East-West relations, many Americans and others came to think instead in terms of limited cooperation between the superpowers. It was mainly in this context that the later notion of crisis management found its place.

Some of the ideas put forward more recently under the heading of crisis management still carry strong traces of the lopsidedness that characterised the notions of both crisis management and condominium in the sixties. Though the criteria for successful crisis management may now be defined in terms of the interest of international society as a whole, bias has not always been avoided in the application of such criteria. Sometimes exercises in crisis management have been held to have furthered such abstracts as peace, stability, order and justice when the outcome has seemed to favour the political interests of the West. Indeed, it is not unreasonable to suspect that much of the recent scholarly interest in the subject, in America and elsewhere, has been inspired to some extent by a run of international crises settled in favour of the United States and its allies. If the major crises of the sixties had been terminated to the clear advantage of the Soviet Union, some Western writers might have been less impressed with improvements in the technique of crisis management.

But there are points other than that of political bias to be made against the current concept of crisis management. Some of its proponents, it could be argued, have at times failed to make a clear enough distinction between their own observations and generalisations about the conduct of decision-makers in crisis situations and the actual motivations and principles of action of the actors concerned. There may have been a tendency to reason that, since a number of international crises have been overcome in a certain way, the governments of the principal powers must have been guided by certain methods of managing crises. But can we be sure that the supposed progress from unconscious to conscious crisis management actually has taken place, that the so-called techniques of crisis management in fact have gained acceptance? Though it may be possible to discern symmetric patterns in the interaction of the superpowers in some past crises, it is very doubtful that all of the statesmen involved—Khrushchev and Kennedy, Kosygin and Johnson, Brezhnev and Nixon—actually saw themselves as partners in crisis management. Even when they appeared to be engaging in exercises in dual crisis management, it is questionable that they really knew what they were doing. It seems likely that at least some of the various subtle techniques of managing crisis which are said to have played a part in the successful handling of particular situations of conflict were developed largely unintentionally and applied more or less unconsciously.

Coral Bell draws attention to this possibility in her essay *The Conventions of Crisis*.[3] Presenting ambiguity in signalling as an important technique of crisis management, she suggests that it largely accounted for the American success in the handling of the Taiwan Strait crisis of 1958. But she goes on to wonder whether Dulles was actually aware of engaging in a creative use of ambiguity when he matched Eisenhower's mild and seemingly conciliatory statements with his own tough and intransigent signals. Another successful technique of management, Coral Bell suggests, is to turn what she calls an adversary crisis into an intramural one. But again, while agreeing that a transformation of this kind has taken place in a number of cases and has been of some importance in shaping the course of crises, one may question whether the policy-makers involved were actually conscious at the time of applying a technique of crisis management. The same sort of question arises in connection with part of Oran Young's work on international crises.[4] In some of the cases where he detects 'tacit coordination' of super-power efforts, others may see only parallel but separate steps, or the spontaneous action-reaction relationship characteristic of rivalry with restraint.

A further query worth raising concerns the notion of crisis itself. Some of those who commend crisis management as one of the more promising techniques of modern statecraft seem inclined to assume that an international crisis is generally treated as an unwelcome emergency. They tend to present the phenomenon as one which the decision-maker suddenly and unexpectedly comes up against and to which he has to react as best he can. Coral Bell makes a striking comparison with the case of a car in a skid, the implication presumably being that the statesman, like the driver of the skidding car, will do what he can to save the situation and bring things back to normal. But, of course, international crises are not always like that. The distinction made in some of the literature on the subject between a precipitated and an encountered crisis recognises that international crises may be preferred instruments of policy. Certainly, Bismarck deliberately used crisis as a way of achieving what he wanted ('war scares' they were called in those days). Khrushchev, too, sometimes employed crisis as an instrument of conducting foreign policy. And Nixon occasionally did the same in the context of the war in Indochina. Naturally, statesmen who consciously use crises to further their ends have to exercise a good deal of control to prevent events from taking a self-defeating course; but their role as crisis managers is rather different from that of statesmen who find themselves faced with an unintentional and unwanted crisis.

There are also situations in which a party to a crisis, even though it has not itself brought the crisis about, still finds it not entirely unwelcome. If a government regards a crisis encountered as a challenge or even as an opportunity, it will be bound to concentrate on defending or pursuing its own interests in the conflict. The reactions of the superpowers to the Middle Eastern crisis of 1967, especially those of the United States, were largely of this nature. Those who feel compelled to use crises, whether precipitated or encountered, in an attempt to improve the position of their own side in an international conflict can hardly be trusted at the same time to manage crises in the interest of international society as a whole. The fact that crises in relations between the superpowers are generated more often than not by one side or the other for purposes of its own, and are used by each to further its own interests at the expense of the other, seems to undermine at least the more optimistic notions of dual crisis management.

Behind some current thinking about the conduct of great powers in situations of crisis there may lurk a misconception of the nature of international crisis. Perhaps a lingering notion of crisis as an unnecessary evil, probably stemming from the old liberal internationalist assumption of a basic harmony in international relations, has given rise to an expectation that, given good will on both sides, the governments of the principal powers will be able to control the crises arising in their relations. Some writers may even hope that one day in the not too distant future it will be possible to move from crisis management to crisis avoidance. But international crises are integral parts of an on-going, never-ending conflict. Clausewitz's best-known dictum about war applies to crisis too, in the sense that there is no break in the continuity of conflict and no basic change in the attitude of the actors. To say that there are no crises, only a continuum of conflict and diplomacy, is an extreme way of making the same point. In order to isolate crises and subject them to scholarly study, some writers have tried to define, or describe, the phenomenon and to delimit particular crises in time; the difficulties which they have encountered emphasise the need to accept crisis as an inseparable part of the natural conflict of international relations.[5]

In the preceding chapters I have examined the conduct and interaction of the United States and the Soviet Union in four characteristic situations of crisis, namely Suez 1956, Taiwan Strait 1958, Cuba 1962 and the Middle East 1967. The aim has been to find out where the balance between rivalry and cooperation lay in the relationship of the superpowers and, in particular, to discover how close they came to exercising what has been called joint crisis management.

In a dualistic system of international politics, such as that which existed in the fifties and sixties, the two principal powers may attempt to manage an international crisis in two different ways. They may bring pressure to bear on third parties directly involved in the conflict and they may take steps to control rivalry between themselves. Though in both cases the motivation of the two powers will be the same, namely to avoid general war, it will be convenient for analytical purposes to consider the efforts of the Soviet Union and the United States under these two headings.

The various conceivable types of dual efforts to manage crises by influencing third parties may be arranged according to the degree of cooperation between the two principal powers. The very minimum would be that of parallel but unconcerted and uncoordinated steps. Whether unconsciously or consciously, the two governments may follow similar lines in their measures to restrain the parties directly involved in the conflict. In all the four crises considered here this happened to some extent, though parallel efforts were not in all cases of equal importance in influencing the course of events.

In the Suez crisis, dual pressure on the parties involved was a significant feature and played an important part in terminating the crisis. After the Israeli action, the initiatives of the superpowers in the United Nations followed similar lines; and before 6 November and in the subsequent weeks, the influence they brought to bear on Britain, France and Israel had the same aims, namely to stop the Suez action and secure a withdrawal of forces. Though the private economic and diplomatic pressures from Washington were more important than the public military threats from Moscow, both played a part.

In the Taiwan Strait crisis of 1958, too, parallel but un-coordinated efforts by the superpowers were a feature, though they played a less important role. The Soviet Government probably encouraged the Chinese to exercise caution at certain critical junctures of the crisis, though it is not clear how much pressure was required to restrain the Chinese, who may have been cautious anyway. The American government urged the Nationalist Chinese to accept restraint in particular issues, but was not very successful, apart from preventing the Nationalists from bombing the mainland.

Parallel restraint was very important in the Cuban missile crisis at the end of the confrontation stage and in the aftermath. The crisis was terminated by each of the superpowers checking its Cuban allies, the Soviet Union by withdrawing its weapons and the United States by agreeing, in effect, not to sponsor an invasion of Cuba.

In each of the three major phases of the crisis in the Middle East in 1967, the superpowers took some steps to moderate the conduct of the parties. By private warnings or assurances and sometimes by public appeals, they tried to restrain the Arabs and Israelis in order, first, to stave off war, then to bring it to an end, and finally, to prevent its recurrence. But, on the whole, they were unsuccessful. The Soviet Union and the United States exercised less control over the local protagonists in this coflict than in any of the three previous crises considered here.

At a slightly more advanced stage of dual efforts at crisis management of this type, the powers not only take parallel and separate measures to restrain the allies or clients directly involved but also urge or warn each other to do so. The parallelism of influence on third parties is reinforced by a mutuality of pressure between the principal powers. Both of them strive to maintain the duality of restraining interference, without, however, coordinating their efforts.

The Suez crisis is not an example of this. Since the pressures of both superpowers were directed at the allies and friends of the United States, the demand for restraining influence could hardly be mutual. While the Soviet government was free to call for joint military action, the American government was in no position to urge the rival to exert influence on Britain, France and Israel.

In the other three crises, however, each of the superpowers urged the other to control or restrain its side. In the Taiwan Strait crisis Khrushchev called on, and apparently also warned, the Americans to keep a tight rein on Nationalist Chinese forces, while Eisenhower appealed to the Russians to pacify the Chinese Communists. These mutual appeals had little effect, however, partly because they seemed to be made mainly for propaganda purposes and partly because each power was already doing all it considered necessary or possible in that respect.

During the Cuban missile crisis, this type of exercise in dual crisis management was much more important. The implementation of the agreement reached by the superpowers resulted to a very considerable extent from mutual, though not equal, pressure to check the Cuban allies.

In the Middle Eastern crisis of 1967, such mutuality of pressure, though present, played a smaller role. At every stage of the crisis, each superpower appealed to the other, both in private and in public, to try harder to control its clients; and on 10 June, during the cease-fire negotiations between Syria and Israel, the Soviet Union even put pressure on the United States by threatening to take military measures. But, since attempts to restrain the local parties were largely unsuccessful, these mutual appeals and threats could be of only marginal importance.

An even more advanced stage of dual efforts to restrain third parties is marked by tacit coordination of the measures taken by the principal powers. Here the two powers make a conscious attempt to bring their separate efforts into harmony with each other, without however concerting them through the channels of diplomacy.

The four crises examined here do not provide a variety of examples of this form of crisis management. In the closing stages of the Cuban missile crisis, the superpowers did achieve a degree of reciprocity in their efforts to implement the agreement they had reached. But the imbalance of the relationship between the two powers at this stage of the crisis, when the Americans put very strong pressure on the Soviet government and the Russians responded by putting equally strong pressure on the Cuban government, disturbed the harmony of the process of coordination. If there was tacit coordination of separate efforts in this case, it did not come about through equal and willing interaction.

A higher stage of dual crisis management of this type is that of concerted efforts. Here the two powers coordinate their parallel measures through direct negotiation with each other. Examples of this are about as rare in the four cases examined as those of tacit coordination. But the Middle Eastern crisis of 1967 did produce one or two minor instances of diplomatic cooperation between the superpowers as well as a few half-hearted attempts in the same direction. Thus, on 25 and 26 May, the two governments arranged for their representatives to deliver notes to the governments of both Egypt and Israel urging self-restraint. And the first exchange on the 'hot line' after the outbreak of war contained hints of concerted efforts to influence the two sides. At the United Nations, too, there were signs of a cooperative spirit in superpower relations on the first day of war. But these isolated essays in diplomatic concert had no influence on the course of events, and soon gave way to active rivalry between the superpowers.

The highest conceivable level of dual crisis management, of the type directed at third parties, is that of *joint* diplomatic, or even military, action. None of the crises examined here presents an example of such a degree of superpower cooperation. In the Suez crisis the Soviet Union publicly appealed to the United States to join in a common military action to check the 'aggression', but received the answer that such a course was unthinkable.

Even the Cuban missile crisis failed to produce a real joint effort to impose a settlement. The Americans did not exercise their pressure on Castro *together with* but *through* the Russians, persistently refusing to deal with the Cuban government.

It is reported that the Americans, in their first formal policy meeting after the outbreak of the Six Day War, discussed the possibility of working with the Soviet Union to arrange a cease-fire. But, as we know, such ideas were soon dispelled. None of these crises revealed elements of 'condominium' in the relationship of the superpowers.

Like the five stages of dual efforts to restrain third parties distinguished here, the various conceivable types of dual attempts to control rivalry in the central relationship of a dualistic system may be arranged according to degree of cooperation between the parties.

At the lowest level we have dual but independent self-restraint. At the crucial stages of all the crises considered here, both of the superpowers exercised considerable self-restraint in their relations with each other. In the tense situation that developed in the Suez crisis after 5 November, the Soviet Union avoided putting direct pressure on the United States, threatening only its allies and then hedging this with an appeal for superpower cooperation. The United States responded with carefully measured pressure on the Soviet Union, at the same time exerting strong influence on its own allies as a means of eliminating the dangerous state of affairs.

In the other three situations, which were more clearly East-West crises than Suez and therefore contained higher potential for escalation, dual self-restraint on behalf of the superpowers was of crucial importance in containing the conflicts. Self-restraint in the crisis of 1958 was more conspicuous in the case of the Soviet Union, which for long kept out of the conflict and throughout refrained from taking any physical measures which might have indicated a desire to become involved. But the United States, too, displayed restraint, particularly in its non-violent reactions to the Chinese blockade. It was through self-control more than through any other type of effort by the superpowers to manage this crisis that the conflict was localised and general war averted.

In the case of the Cuban missile crisis, American restraint was most conspicuous in tactics and style. Once the Kennedy administration had decided to have an open confrontation with the Soviet Union, it acted with great caution, choosing the least offensive measures and carrying them out in a manner calculated to avoid violence and escalation. In the confrontation, both sides obviously took much care to limit tension, each concentrating on immediate interests, playing down ideological conflict and using the utmost caution in the interaction in the field.

In the Middle Eastern crisis of 1967, the determination of each superpower not to become involved in hostilities was of decisive importance in localising the conflict.

In none of the four crises, however, did the two powers stop at dual and independent self-restraint. In each case they went at least one step further in their efforts to control the conflict: they urged or warned each other to exercise restraint. Even in the Suez crisis there was a significant element of mutual threat. Though the Soviet pressure was indirect, it did contain a veiled threat of rocket warfare and a more open one of conventional military intervention, which the United States could not ignore any more than could its two European allies. The Americans, seeking to check any possible Soviet aggressive designs, responded by warning of nuclear retaliation and by alerting its forces.

In the two subsequent crises, each side invoked the threat of retaliation in order to prevent the other from extending or escalating the conflict. In the Taiwan Strait crisis a number of statements by prominent Americans, together with the shipment of certain arms to Taiwan, suggested that the United States was prepared to respond with whatever force was necessary to stop Chinese aggression. In the later stage of the crisis, Khrushchev took the step of invoking the nuclear deterrent in his correspondence with Eisenhower. These threats, however, may have been of relatively little importance to the course of events, since all three major powers involved were possibly determined to exercise caution anyway.

In the direct confrontation of the Cuban missile crisis, the threat of retaliation was much more important. In both public and private messages, each of the two leaders declared his intention to retaliate if nuclear weapons were used by the opponent, thus compelling each side not to escalate the conflict to the critical level.

At various stages of the Middle Eastern crisis of 1967, too, the powers encouraged and warned each other to use restraint, which helped to localise the conflict. In the pre-war stage, the determination of each not to intervene militarily in the conflict was bolstered by mutual declarations of support for the clients, and by verbal warnings to each other as well as by naval movements. At the end of the war, Johnson checked Kosygin's threat to intervene militarily to help Syria by ordering a change in the course and position of the Sixth Fleet.

Corresponding to tacit coordination of parallel steps to restrain third parties, we have tacit coordination of measures to reduce tension in the central relationship. This was not a prominent feature of either of the first two crises discussed here, neither of which involved the superpowers to an equal extent and neither of which was resolved through superpower interaction. It was present in the Taiwan Strait crisis, but only in the relationship between the United States and Communist China.

However, in the Cuban missile crisis some form of tacit coordination of measures of self-restraint played an important role in preventing the physical confrontation from getting out of hand. In the crucial stages, the Americans took care to give the Russians good time to think after each move, avoided backing them into a corner and refrained from humiliating exultation, all in order to expedite a Soviet retreat. American management of this type and the Russian response produced a degree of reciprocity in the two governments' steps to limit and reduce tension, but it was not the result of a balanced relationship. The exceedingly strong pressure employed by the Americans and the tactical and strategic disadvantages suffered by the Russians led to an unequal interaction and disharmonious coordination.

In the Middle Eastern crisis, too, there was a significant element of tacit coordination of superpower efforts, which in this case was aimed at avoiding unilateral physical intervention in the conflict. Through Russian responses to a number of American messages over the 'hot line' and various moves in the field, a certain interaction developed at crucial stages of the war. But here, too, the relationship was rather lopsided. Once more the United States enjoyed the upper hand, with the result that the process of coordination again became less than harmonious.

Concerted efforts to restrain third parties correspond to concerted decisions by the two principal powers to stay clear of hostilities between others or negotiated agreement to reduce or eliminate a conflict between themselves. While the Middle Eastern crisis of 1967 presents an example of the former, the Cuban missile crisis illustrates the latter.

The Cuban crisis was settled through an agreement between the superpowers negotiated by the two heads of government, who communicated through public and private, formal and informal channels. But, like the tacit coordination of the measures taken in the field, their negotiations and agreement reflected a superior American pressure. It was dual, but certainly not equal crisis management.

Already at the pre-war stage of the Middle Eastern crisis, the governments of the Soviet Union and the United States, using both formal and informal contacts, managed to communicate to each other their intention not to intervene directly, assuming both took the same line. This agreement was in effect confirmed immediately after the outbreak of war. Over the 'hot line' Kosygin apparently made what could be taken as a suggestion for an informal pact of non-intervention. But, though the superpowers succeeded in concerting their policies to stay out of the war and, thus, in preventing a major war, their agreement probably helped to bring about the local war. The knowledge that the other superpower did not intend to become involved made it seem less imperative for each of them to restrain its clients, less risky for Egypt to persevere with its challenge, and more necessary for Israel to respond with force.

The four crises examined here present no case of joint action by the superpowers to control tension in the central relationship, which would be the highest form of cooperation in crisis management of this type. It is difficult to imagine what form such action could take, unless one would include in this category instances where the two parties jointly referred their issue to a higher body, for example the United Nations. At the Glassboro meeting after the Six Day War, Kosygin did suggest to Johnson that the question of opening the Gulf of Aqaba be referred to the International Court of Justice. But even if the Americans had taken up this suggestion, it would hardly have amounted to a joint effort of the type that conceivably could be directed at third parties involved in a conflict. The idea of two great-power rivals engaging in joint action to control or eliminate an existing conflict between themselves is self-contradictory.

Perhaps further research and analysis of these four and other international crises might lead to some refinements of the distinctions between two types and five degrees of dual crisis management. But the picture is already clear enough to draw a number of conclusions about the dualistic system of the United States and the Soviet Union:

1. Exercises in dual crisis management normally took place, if at all, at the lowest levels of cooperation between the superpowers. In relation to third parties, they mostly assumed the form of parallel and separate efforts to restrain allies or clients, reinforced by mutual appeals and warnings between the principals to use their influence. In relations between the superpowers themselves, dual efforts of crisis management usually took the form of self-restraint on both sides, again backed by mutual encouragement and threat.

2. Dual attempts by the superpowers to restrain third parties involved in conflict were sometimes motivated by competing interests (as in the Suez crisis), were generally accompanied by opposition and rivalry (as, for example, in the Taiwan Strait crisis), and were often eclipsed by tension and conflict between the great

powers themselves (as in the Six Day War).

3. When exercises in dual crisis management reached the more advanced stages of great-power cooperation, taking the forms of tacit coordination or even concerted efforts, they tended to be results of superior pressure brought to bear by one superpower on the other, in which case they reflected conflict and coercion rather than harmony and a will to cooperate.

4. Attempts at *joint* crisis management, in any stricter sense of the term, were rare phenomena.

5. Dual efforts of crisis management were generally negative in their aim, being directed at avoiding major war in the immediate situation, not at settling the underlying issue of the crisis. Only in the termination of the Cuban missile crisis did the powers make some progress in tackling the deeper issues. The crises of 1958 and 1967 were both conspicuous for leaving the issues of the conflict untouched.

6. Although certain facilities for improving the techniques were introduced (especially the 'hot line'), progress in the field of crisis management was not striking in the eleven years between the first and the last of the four crises. Though it was in the later two crises that the more cooperative forms of management were brought into play, this may be not so much a sign of greater determination and increased ability on the part of the superpowers to control the course of crises as a result of the different character of these crises compared with the two earlier ones. While the crisis of 1956 was to a large extent between the United States and its two allies and that of 1958 essentially between the United States and China, those of 1962 and 1967 were both manifestly between the superpowers, the former directly and the latter indirectly. Hence these crises had to be resolved through superpower interaction, which, as we have seen, took a rather unequal form, especially at the confrontation or near-confrontation stages.

In support of the general conclusion that there was rather little progress in the field of dual crisis management, one might mention also the case of a later major international crisis, that of Bangladesh in 1971. This crisis, though not strictly comparable to the four earlier cases discussed, was hardly an impressive example of dual superpower management. As in 1967, the contribution of the United States and the Soviet Union as crisis managers consisted mainly in keeping out of the hostilities.

The handling of the next major crisis, that of the Middle East in

1973, seems a much more striking case of superpower management. At first sight, it might be taken to indicate considerable progress in dual crisis management. But this crisis is even less comparable to the four situations of dualistic conflict examined here than was the Bangladesh crisis. Whereas the crisis of 1971 took place when the global great-power triangle was barely past the embryonic stage, the later Middle-Eastern crisis erupted in a much more fully developed triangular situation. Though the former crisis, like that of the Taiwan Strait in 1958, involved all of the three principal powers, from some points of view it could still be seen mainly in the context of the declining dualistic system. But the crisis of 1973, though it, like that of 1967, was essentially between the Soviet Union and the United States, must be understood in terms of triangular dynamics. Whatever the degree of coordination of Russo-American efforts to control events before, during and after the October War, whatever the extent of Soviet support for American attempts to terminate the crisis, the interaction of the superpowers must be related to the conflict between the Soviet Union and China and to their competition for diplomatic support from the United States. Once the rapprochement between Peking and Washington had made a Sino-American entente a possibility which no Soviet government could ignore, the Soviet Union was bound to feel less free than under the dualistic system to obstruct American efforts to manage crises and control conflict, in the Middle East and elsewhere.

The conduct of the superpowers in the four situations of crisis referred to here suggests that it is misleading to present them as partners in crisis management. Rather, it seems, they should be seen as rivals engaged in continuous struggle, but a struggle which is subject to certain restraints. To put it another way, the relationship between the Soviet Union and the United States has been characterised by restrained conflict rather than by limited cooperation.

The experience and prudence of the superpowers have inhibited them from engaging each other in a constant and unmitigated duel. While the habits and norms of traditional diplomatic intercourse among states have encouraged them to look for areas of agreement, the danger of a major nuclear war has compelled them to restrict their hostility. In the course of the prolonged conflict and repeated crises of the Cold War. the two powers seem somehow to have developed a number of general principles as well as various sets of loose rules for regulating their struggle. On the basis of their conduct in the four crises examined here, it is possible to make a tentative list of some of the principles that may have come to guide their interaction:

1. Do not intervene militarily in each other's established spheres of influence. This rule, which was respected by the Americans in various crises in Eastern Europe (for example those over Hungary in 1956 and Czechoslovakia in 1968) and by the Russians when the United States intervened in the Dominican Republic in 1965, was tested and confirmed in the Cuban missile crisis.

2. As a corollary of the first rule: pursue your keenest rivalry in the 'grey zones' of the world rather than on the fringes of the better demarcated spheres of influence. The Middle East remains a principal area of conflict and competition between the two powers.

3. Prefer conflict by proxy rather than the more dangerous path of direct confrontation. This must have been the chief lesson of Cuba.

4. Encourage your allies or clients only up to the point where the danger of major war becomes real; then check them—if you can. The crises of 1958, 1962 and 1967 all showed such reversals in the relationships with the third parties.

5. Urge or compel your rival to restrain his protégés as well. This rule was followed in the same three crises.

6. Do not intervene militarily in a local conflict if the rival might feel compelled to follow. This rule was respected by both powers in the crisis of 1967.

7. Urge or compel the rival to stay out of a local conflict if you might feel compelled to follow if he intervenes. This rule, too, was observed during the Six Day War.

8. In a direct confrontation with the other superpower, exercise the greatest self-restraint. This means concentrating on immediate interests, choosing the minimum measures required for any purpose, not overreacting to the steps taken by the opponent, exercising strict control over the forces in the field, not indulging in ideological debate, not triumphing at signs of retreat by the opponent, etc.— in short, taking care not to escalate the conflict. These maxims have been deduced mainly from the handling of the Cuban missile crisis, especially President Kennedy's part in it, but may be detected, too, in reactions to near-confrontation situations which occurred in some other crises.

9. The complementary rule in a direct confrontation is to take all

possible and necessary steps to urge or compel the opponent to use self-restraint. This may mean, on the one hand, discouraging him from escalating the conflict and, on the other, encouraging him to back down or to engage in a reciprocal process of reducing tension. The Cuban case, too, provides the best example of this rule in operation.

10. If necessary, invoke the threat of nuclear retaliation to deter the opponent from attacking your allies or yourself with nuclear weapons. The Americans invoked the deterrent during the Suez crisis to counter the Russian veiled threats of rocket attacks on Britain and France; and the Russians invoked it during the Taiwan Strait crisis to protect its ally against what Khrushchev called 'atomic blackmail'. Both powers threatened retaliation with nuclear weapons during the Cuba crisis to deter each other from escalating the conflict to the strategic nuclear level.

In addition to such rather general principles of strategy, there appears to be a variety of ill-defined rules, or vague guidelines, relating to particular situations of conflict or to special spheres of rivalry. These, which have been described as 'ground rules' (Henry Pachter), 'operational rules' (Hedley Bull) and 'rules of the game' (Richard Falk), may rest on mutual understandings or tacit agreements between the superpowers. Some may apply, for example, to particular types of situations of international crisis. Thus, there seems to be a general understanding between the United States and the Soviet Union that they communicate with each other over the 'hot line' when a crisis in their relationship reaches a certain danger level. Other sets of rules may refer to special types or particular areas of conflict. Examples of the former kind may be found in various guidelines assumed to regulate superpower rivalry in connection with civil strife in third countries. To find illustrations of the latter sort of rules, one might look at the rivalry in the Middle East or the war in Indochina, both of which are likely to have produced a number of informal agreements between the superpowers to regulate their own interaction as well as their relations with the respective protégés.

A careful effort to identify and investigate such rules would be of more than academic interest. To clarify the nature and role of the various sets of tacit understandings and informal agreements between the superpowers, one would have to explore the logical and psychological subtleties of games. Among the questions to be answered would be the following: how do rules of this type come about? On what degrees of agreement may they rest? How and, especially, to what extent do they influence the conduct of the superpowers in their competitive interaction? The last question is the crucial one. Assumptions based on past behaviour may prove invalid in new situations. Guidelines laid down in periods of détente may disappear when tension reaches a climax. Rules may be changing even before they have been quite spelt out and fully understood.

Neither the general principles nor the specific guidelines to regulate struggle between the superpowers can be binding or immutable. As they are developed and tested in conflict, so they may be challenged and changed in crisis. The game may be subject to rules, but the rules are conditional on the game.

The current transformation of the international system creates further uncertainty about the application of the loose principles and informal rules tentatively outlined here. Most of the tacit under-standings and mutual expectations on which they rest were formed during the later years of the Cold War and the earlier stage of the East-West détente, when the political structure of the global system was essentially dualistic. Now, when the diplomatic ascent of China, and the rise of other major powers, is bringing about a more complex situation, both the basis and the role of the old habits of restraint must be changing. The extent to which such principles and rules can still play a part in limiting international conflict will depend on a number of factors.

On the one hand, some solid reasons may be advanced for maintaining that the various diplomatic devices developed by the superpowers for restraining themselves and their protégés in situations of conflict may be almost as relevant and important in the new pattern of international tension as they have been in the old. First, despite the rapid development of a triangular system and various signs of the emergence of an even more complex structure, the *central* relationship is still dualistic, and likely to remain so for some considerable time. Though today the centre of friction, as it has been put, may be between the Soviet Union and China, the centre of tension is still between the two powers that command overwhelming nuclear force. To regulate their relationship is as important as ever. Second, a triangular system is made up of three dual relationships (a triad being the only group in which the number of relationships is equal to the number of parties). A strategy of conflict created by the first and most important pair of powers is likely to have at least some influence on the conduct of the other two relationships. On these grounds it may be safely concluded that a study of the various principles and rules of international conflict developed, so laboriously and so precariously, by the two superpowers must be of more than historical interest.

On the other hand, there are good reasons for suspecting that shared habits of restraint of the sort that the superpowers may have acquired are going to be an even less reliable means of controlling international conflict in the triangular system than they have been in the dualistic. First, there is the difficulty of securing a degree of agreement among all of the three powers on the principles and guidelines to be followed. This is not just a matter of the extent to which China may be prepared to play the game according to rules agreed by the two other powers, but also a question of whether the Soviet Union and the United States will be willing to adjust their rules to suit the requirements of China. The war in Vietnam, when more is known of the secret great-power diplomacy surrounding it, should provide much material to illustrate the difficulties involved in such a process of mutual adjustment within a triangular pattern of conflict. Second, there may be forces inherent in the dynamics of the triangular system which militate against a successful trilateral control of conflict. It is possible that conflict may be restrained on one side of the triangle at the expense of the other two sides, or on two sides at the expense of the third. To appreciate the difficulties of regulating international conflict in the new system and to explore ways of overcoming them, it is necessary to analyse the dynamics of the great-power triangle.

In the remaining chapters, I shall examine first the simple triangle of the United States, the Soviet Union and China and then consider the more complex structure that will appear when other major powers establish themselves in the emerging global system.

PART TWO
THE TRIANGULAR SYSTEM

6 The Simple Triangle

The first question worth asking about the so-called triangular system of the United States, the Soviet Union and China is whether or not it exists. Is the dominant relationship of contemporary international politics triangular? If so, is it a system?

The central relationship of international politics is still dualistic. It rests on the strategic dominance of the two superpowers and their long tradition of exclusive interaction, culminating in the SALT agreements. It is maintained as well by the other members of the states system accepting the superiority of the United States and the Soviet Union. Even China, by insisting that there are only two superpowers in the world and by denying any ambition on its own part to become a third, testifies that these two powers are in a class by themselves.

In recent years, however, there have been signs that a multiple system comprising more than three powers may be emerging. Japan has been developing relations with both the Soviet Union and China. Western Europe, through moves towards a withdrawal of superpower forces in Western and Eastern Europe and the convening of a European security conference as well as through its economic progress and sporadic efforts in the direction of political integration, has been seeking more freedom of action on the international scene. Even India, having won hegemony in South Asia, may be preparing itself for a future great-power role beyond its region.

Is there, between the dualistic balance of power still with us and a much more complex system not yet crystallised, a *triangular* relationship of some significance? Or, to put it another way, is China in a class different from that of Japan and Western Europe? It seems that it is. The reason why Japan cannot yet be classed with China in the hierarchy of powers is not merely that it lacks nuclear weapons, though this is important, but also that it lags far behind China in its willingness to assume an independent role in global politics. Till well into the present decade, Japan clung to the bipolar view of the world, ignoring many of the signs that it was breaking down. By concentrating exclusively on its alliance with the United States, it postponed the difficult choice between the Soviet Union and China. The so-called 'Nixon shocks', the announcements by the United States of the opening of relations with China and of the new economic policy in 1971, were apparently real shocks in Japan. Only since then, it seems, has that country begun seriously to explore the possibility of a more complex structure of international politics.

Western Europe, too, through its NATO links, is still closely identified with one of the superpowers. It is also far from having enough political cohesion to play an independent part at the highest level in a complex balance of power. And India, whose leaders since Nehru have denied entertaining any ambition for a great-power role, is likely to remain for a long time yet preoccupied with domestic affairs and relations within the sub-continent.

China, on the other hand, has long played an autonomous part in world politics. Ever since it publicly liberated itself from its dependence on the Soviet Union, it has challenged the supremacy of the two superpowers. Building up its already very considerable stock of nuclear weapons and still relying on its ideological appeal, it looks more and more like a power capable one day of playing an almost equal part at the highest level. Despite its disclaimers, China seems on the way to joining the club of superpowers.

In 1971 China—for long involved with the Soviet Union, first as ally, then as near-enemy and more recently as rival—completed the triangle by responding to American overtures. The triangle formed by these powers, though possibly representing only a stage in a transition from the duel of the Soviet Union and the United States to a complex system of more than three powers, may be the dominant relationship of the late seventies and early eighties. Perhaps it will survive long enough for us to gain a better understanding of the nature of great-power triangles.

Is this triangular relationship a system? Sometimes when we speak of systems in international politics we refer to a structure based on well-defined principles or rules which are consciously followed by the parties concerned for the sake of agreed ends. The European Congress System of the restoration period after the Napoleonic Wars was of this type. Through the practice of regular reunions (what we would now call summit meetings), the great powers managed European politics by concerted diplomacy and

occasionally even joint action, their aim being to maintain the
Vienna settlement in general and the Bourbon restoration in
particular. Clearly, the triangle of America, Russia and China is not
a system of this order. It lacks a formal basis and has no defined
rules. Nor has it existed long enough for all of the three parties to
develop tacit principles and informal rules, of the sort discussed in
the previous chapter, to guide their mutual interaction and their
conduct towards other states.

It is not even certain that all of the actors, or indeed any of them,
think in terms of triangularity. The United States, according to
various public statements by President Nixon and Dr Kissinger and
succeeding policy-makers, has focused on the long-term aim of a
complex balance of five great powers, although its policy towards
China indicates that it may see a triangular relationship as a step
towards that goal. The Soviet Union, which has a much stronger ·
interest than the United States in keeping down China and for
which the Sino-American rapprochement must have been a major
diplomatic defeat, has not embraced the triangular idea with
enthusiasm. About China's attitude one can only speculate. If
China's move towards the United States was dictated largely by fear
of the Soviet Union, it is just possible that it still sees the world as
being dominated by only two great powers, one of which seems
more dangerous than the other. If, on the other hand, the move was
motivated by fear of both the Soviet Union and Japan, and perhaps
of a future alliance of these two traditional enemies of China, then it
may already be well on the way towards conceiving of world politics
in terms of a multiple system of more than three great powers.
Judging by many public statements in past years, it does seem more
likely, however, that China's principal concern is to break up the
exclusive relationship between the two superpowers by strengthening its own position towards each of them, that its aim, in other
words, is to transform the simple constellation into a triangle in
which it occupies one of the corners itself. But if we accept that at
least some of the leaders of China have been thinking in terms of a
triangle, it must be remembered that all such Chinese notions, of
course, are subject to the Communist philosophy of tactics and
strategy and means and ends, and that the ultimate goal is still
world revolution.[1]

Yet, even though the three powers seem to have neither common
aims nor agreed principles, and even if they do not all conceive of
international politics primarily in terms of a triangle, they are still

able to engage in continuous triangular interaction. However different their subjective notions of foreign policy and great-power diplomacy may be, objectively the three actors form a system in the more limited sense of maintaining an observable pattern of interrelation, a pattern which stands out from the rest of the international relations of the world. The longer the triangular relationship lasts and the more conscious the parties become of acting within it, the more likely it is that this system will undergo some development. Eventually it could conceivably take on some of the qualities of a system in the more advanced sense of the term. For the purpose of the present analysis, it will be assumed that the newly established system of three great powers will survive and develop for some time. This will allow us to enquire, first, into the character of the triangular relationships that may result and, second, into the way the system will work.

Before discussing the more likely types of triangular relationships, it might be worth dealing briefly with what have been called the absolute solutions of relations between preponderant powers. There are three: withdrawal, condominium and conquest, each of which would put an end to the triangular system.

In earlier times, when empires were separated by large tracts of undefined territory, it sometimes happened apparently that two or more dominant powers which had become exhausted from struggle and rivalry or had become absorbed in domestic affairs backed down and withdrew from interaction with each other. This does not seem a likely outcome in the contemporary situation. Even if the United States experienced a new and more serious wave of social and political unrest, if the Soviet Union became preoccupied with its nationalities problems, and if China underwent another cultural revolution, it is almost inconceivable that they would stop interacting with each other. In a situation marked by a high degree of domestic absorption on the part of each power, one could certainly expect a reduction in the intensity of interaction; but the social, economic, political and strategic interdependence of the modern world would make it very difficult for a group of great powers to contract out completely. If domestic unrest within only one of the countries brought it close to civil war, that power might well react by making a temporary and partial withdrawal from the international scene, which would tend to alter the structure of the triangular system and push it in the direction of the dualistic pattern. At present, a social upheaval in China, perhaps following a renewed struggle for political leadership, seems the least unlikely event to produce such a result.

For reasons gone into elsewhere,[2] a condominium of the three seems almost as unlikely as mutual withdrawal. A study of past relations between empires or great powers suggests that condominium, in the sense of joint government of the political world or a large part of it, is an exceptional type of arrangement, even in dualistic situations. Normally brief and unstable, it is generally marked by tension and rivalry between the partners while it lasts. That the United States, the Soviet Union and China might be able to overcome their mutual suspicions and agree on lines of territorial division and terms of diplomatic cooperation is difficult to believe. They would not only have to demarcate spheres of separate influence and areas of joint responsibility but would also have to concert their diplomacy or even act jointly to deal with particular situations. A concert merely to control nuclear weapons, itself very difficult to set up in a triangular situation, would not amount to condominium of the world.

Three possibilities of conquest may be distinguished in a triad of powers: by one of two; by two of one; and by one of one. In a paper on triangles and duels read to the British Committee on the Theory of International Politics in 1972, Martin Wight said, 'Triangles, like duels, are relationships of conflict, and are resolved by war. The triangle of Russia, China and the United States has not yet been so resolved, but the historical precedents permit no other generalisation.'[3] He went on to classify triangles on the model of a knockout tournament, distinguishing 'preliminary round', 'first round', the 'semi-final', and the 'end-game' or 'world championship'. Though the generalisation may be justified by history, it does not necessarily apply to the present triangle. While China is clearly unable to knock out the two superpowers, the balance of nuclear deterrence seems likely to prevent both the Soviet Union and the United States from attempting to destroy the two rivals. Nor can we be certain that the triangle will be resolved through one of the other two ways of conquest.

If conquest by one power over two leads towards world hegemony, that by two powers over one leaves a dualistic situation. In present circumstances, this solution seems little more likely than the previous one. Deterrence stands in the way of any attempt by the other two to eliminate either the Soviet Union or the United States. Nor is there much prospect of China becoming the victim of an aggressive alliance of the two superpowers. Since the Soviet Union and the United States never joined each other to destroy China during the sixties and early seventies, when China was obviously the potential challenger to their dual hegemony and when its relative weakness would have made it an easier victim of conquest, they are hardly likely to do so now, when China's military strength is much more impressive, and after the SALT agreements, according to some interpretations of their significance, have reduced its strategic inferiority by limiting the defensive capabilities of the superpowers.

Conquest by one over one is perhaps a more likely way of resolving the triangle. The mutual deterrence of the superpowers makes China the most obvious candidate for elimination. Yet this solution seems less possible now than it did in the late sixties, when many feared that the Soviet Union would launch a pre-emptive strike against China's growing nuclear rocket capability. It did not do so (just as the United States did not do it to the Soviet Union when the Russians were in the early stage of *their* development of nuclear weapons); and the SALT agreements, as far as one can see, tend to make it less likely that the Soviet Union will attempt it in future. What is more, the longer the triangular system exists, and the more each of the three parties comes to think in terms of triangularity, the more probable it is that the outsider in such a contest would at least threaten to support the potential victim of a knock-out blow, in order to avoid the possibility of an ensuing dual with the victor. There were already signs of this line in the American reactions to the war scare between the Soviet Union and China in 1969.

All of the solutions outlined here are absolute in the sense that they would amount to a dissolution of the triangular system. Withdrawal would put a stop to interaction; condominium would tend to unite the exercise of power; and conquest would transform the system into a dualistic or a unifocal structure. Consistent with the assumption that the triangular system has a future, such solutions will be excluded from further consideration here.

For the purpose of examining the less conclusive relationships possible among three great powers, a distinction might be made between those which describe an equilateral triangle and those which produce a lopsided situation, a state in which not all the three sides are similar. In the former class, three types of triangular relationships may be distinguished, namely concert of three, trilateral conflict, and a trilateral mixture of cooperation and conflict.

A concert is marked by a high degree of coordination or cooperation in diplomacy, through not so high as that characteristic of a condominium. In a concert, the powers try to manage international politics by habitually consulting each other and by occasionally concerting their measures. They do not go so far as attempting to govern the world by regularly engaging in joint action. Since they can keep a greater distance from each other than the partners to a condominium, who have to identify with each other's policies, a concert may be easier to bring about than a condominial arrangement. Many Western writers of the sixties and seventies, as we have seen, have advocated a concert of the world as a possible and desirable goal for the great powers.[4]

Yet a concert does not seem the most likely outcome of the great-power relations of the seventies. Except for the existence of a substantial shared danger, namely the risk of a major nuclear war, the conditions that in the past have proved essential for the emergence of concert do not seem to be present today.[5] A concert of great powers is usually a post-war phenomenon. Often arising from a war-time coalition, it generally expresses a universal weariness of war as well as a number of common concerns relating to the peace settlement. Normally, it is fairly short-lived. Altogether, it seems to hold out little more hope than does condominium.

At the opposite end of the spectrum of possible relations in a triangular system, we have unmitigated trilateral rivalry. This is a state of affairs in which each power rivals the other two at a high level of intensity, without however entering into the sort of all-out war that could lead to a complete defeat of one or two of the powers. Such a set of relationships seems as unlikely as concert. Just as the three powers whose relations we are considering have too many conflicts of interest and ideology to allow them to enter into close concert, so they have enough in common to stop them from engaging in all-out rivalry. In addition to the paramount common need to avoid nuclear war, they may share a concern to keep down those major powers which could prove a threat to their supremacy. The more the three powers come to accept the triangular system, the more keenly aware they may become of sharing such an interest. The advantages to be derived from the nascent and rather uncertain practice of limited cooperation in special fields, initiated so laboriously by the two superpowers, tends to inhibit the three powers further from entering into unlimited rivalry. What is more, the very dynamics of the triangular system, as will be explained later, contains a force which, if it does not actually make for a degree of cooperation among the parties, then at least imposes some restraints on their altercations.

Much more likely than either the tentative cooperation of concert or the unmitigated rivalry at the other extreme would seem to be the last of the three equilateral types of relationships considered here, namely a trilateral mixture of cooperation and conflict, perhaps resembling that which developed between the Soviet Union and the United States during the sixties. As has been the case in the diplomatic interaction of those two powers, the element of nascent cooperation, tacit coordination, or mutual restraint in such a set of relationships, however one assesses it, would be likely to stem mainly from the need to avoid major war, and to take the form of loosely defined principles and informal rules for regulating the conflicts. How pronounced this positive component of the relationships could become would depend on the extent to which the very substantial difficulties of reaching agreement on guidelines for interaction in a situation of triangular conflict, to which reference was made at the end of the first part of the book, could be overcome.

The element of rivalry, too, may follow the pattern of interaction developed in the earlier dualistic situation. Arthur Burns, in an analysis of the effects of the SALT agreements, has drawn attention to the inclination of the Soviet Union and the United States to export their conflict.[6] This is a tendency which predates the SALT period and which may well be continued in the triangular system. Since the Cold War, there has been a propensity for conflict between the great powers to take the form less and less of direct confrontation and more and more of indirect clash. In Soviet-American relations, it could be argued, there has been a shift from confrontation in Central Europe, where Warsaw Pact and NATO forces used to face each other, for example in various Berlin crises, to crisis or 'war by proxy' in the Middle East. In Sino-Soviet relations the movement has been from direct clash along the common border in Central Asia to rivalry and war between allies or friends in the sub-continent and South East Asia. Even in the history of Sino-American relations one may note the same tendency when comparing the Korean War and the Taiwan Strait crises, which were cases of open war and direct confrontation, with the war in Indochina, to which the one great power never committed troops and from which the other eventually withdrew them. The tacit rule of preferring indirect conflict to the more dangerous path of direct confrontation may already guide not only the rivalry of the Soviet Union and the United States but also the relationships on the other two sides of the triangle.

If such a set of mixed relationships were to last for any length of time, the overall pattern of conflict in the equilateral triangle might thus be one in which the three parties tried to respect each other's minimum spheres of interests and concentrated their rivalries in the so-called grey areas of the world such as the Middle East, the Indian Ocean and Africa, where spheres of influence are not clearly demarcated. Periods of high tension in the system would be likely to alternate with periods of détente. Like the three characters in Sartre's play *Huis Clos*, the powers might sometimes move closer together and sometimes farther apart, without breaking loose from their triangular relationship.

The lopsided triangular situations to be considered here are two-fold: where two powers cooperate against one, and where two powers engage each other in conflict while the third keeps a distance. In the triangle of the United States, the Soviet Union and China, it is possible to imagine at least three sorts of division between two and one. First, there is the possibility of a conflict between the two communist countries and the principal capitalist nation of the world; second, between the two have-states and the one have-not state; and third, between two *status quo* powers and one expansionist power.

A conflict of the first sort, along traditional ideological lines, dominated international politics before the Sino-Soviet split. Whether some time in the future, perhaps after the leadership in Moscow, too, has changed, the two former allies may find it possible to patch up their present conflicts of interests and ideology is difficult to say. But it is worth noting that, according to reports, Lin Piao, and probably other Chinese leaders as well, may have favoured just such a course, and that more recently Teng Hsiao-ping has gone as far as arguing that the danger of war with the Soviet Union is not immediate.

A conflict of the second type, between the two nuclear and economic have-states and China, has been latent during the period of détente between the Soviet Union and the United States, especially in the eyes of the Chinese. Whether that division will be softened or in fact accentuated by Chinese efforts to catch up depends largely on whether or not the two established superpowers will relinquish their dualistic conception of global politics in favour of a triangular one.

A conflict of the third sort, following the rules of the balance of power, might come about if two of the powers saw themselves threatened by an expansion in the influence of the third. If, for example, a Soviet build-up in the Indian Ocean, a general strengthening of its position in the Asian sub-continent and a more active involvement in the affairs of Africa came to be seen by both the Chinese and the Americans as a serious challenge to them and a threat to the global balance of power, it is very possible that China and the United States might move closer together in defence of the *status quo*. Whether the three powers divided on ideological grounds, along have and have-not lines or according to balance-of-power principles, the problem would be one of controlling conflict and managing crises in a struggle between two and one.

The other non-equilateral triangle is that in which two of the parties are involved in intense rivalry with each other. Here the third power tends to assume the role of *tertius gaudens*, the glad third, the merry outsider.[7] If, for example, the area of maximum tension and friction in the emerging system were Europe or the Middle East, as it often was during the Cold War, China would be *tertius gaudens*. If, on the other hand, it were the Far East or South East Asia, the Soviet Union could be the beneficiary. And if it were along the border between the Soviet Union and China or in South Asia, the United States would be in the favoured position.

In such a position, the third party may take various stances. It may encourage both protagonists to pursue their rivalry in order to maintain its own advantage, or it may attempt to mediate between them in order to avoid a major war and a collapse of the system; it may balance the conflict by supporting one side more than the other, or it may stay aloof. Whichever line the third power takes, its relations with both of the others will be better than their relations with each other. Since the essential conflict within such a triangle is between two powers only, the lessons of the Cold War and détente periods of the dualistic system cannot be irrelevant to attempts by the protagonists to keep their rivalry under control, even though the presence of the third party in the system complicates the situation.

If we conclude that the relationships most likely to arise in the triangle of the Soviet Union, the United States and China would be mixtures of cooperation and conflict, whether of the equilateral kind or of the two non-equilateral types distinguished here, we are left with the question of how the triangular system would work. What would be its dynamics? One way of seeking the answer is to start with the equilateral situation and ask which are the forces that help to maintain this state and which the forces that tend to upset it.

If the two principal alternatives to the equilateral situation are that in which two collude against the third and that in which two oppose each other while the third enjoys the part of *tertius gaudens*, then each of the powers in an equilateral triangle may be expected to be motivated, on the one hand, by fear of becoming the victim of a hostile coalition of the other two and, on the other, by a desire to become the third party in a conflict between the other two. These concerns seem likely to encourage each of the three parties, on the one hand, to try to keep on relatively good terms with both of the others and, on the other, to do what it can to stir up and maintain antagonism between them. If each of the three follows both of these lines of action, and if they are all more or less equally successful in their pursuits, the equilateral state of the triangle may be maintained, and the mixture of conflict and cooperation, tension and détente, may be preserved throughout the system.

The element of conflict on each of the three sides of such a triangle will stem partly from the natural clash of interests between the two parties and partly from the efforts of the third party to produce friction in that relationship. The element of détente, or even a degree of cooperation, on each side will spring partly from the general interests of all the powers in avoiding major war and in protecting their system against internal and external challenges and partly from the efforts of each of them to maintain good enough relations with the others to stop them from ganging up against it.

Both of the stabilising forces of the system have been present in the triangle of the United States, the Soviet Union and China since its inception. The tendency for each power to avoid excessive tension in relations with both of the others has been manifested in the Strategic Arms Limitation Talks of the superpowers, in the Warsaw talks between American and Chinese diplomats, and in the Kosygin–Chou negotiations. It may be detected also in various steps taken in the seventies to bring about or to maintain a degree of détente on each side of the triangle: in Europe and the Middle East, in the Far East and South East Asia, and in South Asia. Attempts to control or reduce tension have been more conspicuous in Soviet-American and in Sino-American than in Sino-Soviet relations. In

Europe the superpowers have promoted conferences on security and cooperation and on force reductions, and in the Middle East they have exerted some influence to prevent a flare-up of hostilities. In the Far East the United States and China have reached a rapprochement, and in South East Asia the United States has withdrawn its forces from Vietnam and accepted the victory of communism in Indochina. Such moves by the two pairs of powers, directed as they have been at the four principal centres of great-power tension of the fifties and sixties, may be seen, from one point of view, as attempts to wind up the old East-West issues hanging over from the Cold War of the declining dualistic system in preparation for new patterns of conflict, in other words as part of the process of adjusting to a new system of global politics. From another point of view, however, they may be viewed as part of the dynamics of the emerging system.

The other stabilising tendency, to maintain a beneficial degree of tension between all the parties, has been almost equally noticeable in the present triangle. For more than fifteen years, long before the triangular system took shape, China has tried to put obstacles in the way of what it has described as Russo-American collusion. Certain Soviet moves on the South-East Asian scene in the early-seventies were interpreted as intended to counter steps towards a settlement of Sino-American differences. Since the principal area of open great-power conflict since the emergence of the triangle has been between the Soviet Union and China, it has not been necessary for the United States to make much trouble between them; it has been able to enjoy the position of *tertius gaudens* with relatively little such effort on its part.

The more firmly the triangular system establishes itself, the more pronounced this mischief-making tendency may become. A persistent propensity for any two of the powers to move closer to each other at the expense of others is likely to provoke increasing opposition from both the third power and other states who have an interest in keeping the two apart. Efforts by the third party to maintain a degree of conflict between the potential collaborators may be supported by middle powers and small states caught up between the two great powers and fearing that the cooperation of these may be to the disadvantage of the lesser countries in the region. If Russo-American collaboration became a real threat, Chinese openings towards various East and West European countries might draw a more favourable response. Alternatively, if the Sino-American rapprochement showed signs of developing into an entente, the Soviet Union might find new friends among the South East Asian states.

Yet, though there are forces which may tend to support the equilateral state of the system, it cannot be concluded that the triangle of the great powers is likely to remain in this position of equilibrium. There are also destabilising forces at work. Sources of instability may be found in the uneven composition of the triangle, in its international environment, and in the very dynamics of the system. First, the three powers are not strictly comparable. They are highly idiosyncratic bodies, divided variously along ideological lines, according to level of economic development, and on the basis of strategic capability. To assume that they are both equally willing and equally able to conduct themselves in the manner required to maintain the equilateral equilibrium is quite unrealistic.

Second, there is the influence of forces outside the triangle. For reasons of their own, middle and small powers may sometimes interfere in the system in ways which tend to upset the equilibrium. For the sake of achieving greater clarity in the exposition of the possibilities of the triangle and the dynamics of the system, the effect of outsiders has been largely ignored in the construction of the implicit models employed in this chapter.

Third, there may be something in the dynamics of the triangular system which could make the ability of one power to keep the others apart weaker than the inclination of the others to join against this power. If the most decisive property of any triad is its propensity to divide into a combination of two against one, the writer who at an early stage of the emergence of our great-power triangle predicted a big future for collusion in the new system may well prove right.[8]

The equilibrium of the equilateral triangle is not identical with the balance of power of the triangular system. Considering that the three powers do not have the same goals in world politics and do not command the same amount of resources with which to pursue them, the equidistant situation could quite possibly result in an imbalance of power. In certain conditions, a combination of two against one may well be in accordance with the principles of the balance of power. Collaboration between the Soviet Union and the United States, as economic and strategic have-states, against an aggressive have-not China might be one such situation. Another possibility would be that of the entente between the United States and China, as political *status quo* powers, against a Soviet Union in an expansionist frame of mind. In both cases the balance of power would be on the side of two *status quo* powers which were facing a challenge from a revisionist third party.

In other circumstances, however, a combination of two powers against one may run counter to the balance of power. This would be the case particularly if it were the alliance of two which was revisionist and aggressive. A coalition between a revolutionary China and an expansionist Soviet Union, for example, would tend to upset the balance of the system. Certainly, the Nazi-Soviet pact of 1939 did not make for stability in the composite triangle of the Soviet Union, the Axis powers and the Western powers in Europe before the Second World War. Perhaps therefore, in the last instance, the possibility of the triangular system collapsing in major war cannot be excluded.

The term 'triangular system' has been employed here in three different senses. First, it has been used as a descriptive expression; second, to refer to a set of principles and ideas; and third, as a tool of analysis. The dominant pattern of interaction in contemporary international politics, it has been argued, may be best described as a triangular system, even though its outlines are blurred by the older dualistic pattern, which still lives on, as well as by a more complex pattern which has not yet assumed distinct shape.

At the same time it has been questioned whether all, or indeed any, of the policy-makers of the three principal powers today actually think in terms of a triangular system. Notwithstanding the current pattern of interaction, one may wonder whether the United States, the Soviet Union and China in fact share a set of principles conducive to the maintenance of such a system, or whether their global outlook is still bound by the declining dualistic structure, or even perhaps already becoming influenced by projections of a balance of four, five or six great powers.

Mainly, however, the term has been used as an analytic concept, as a tool for detecting trends in contemporary international politics. The implicit models which have been brought into play for this purpose, though useful for exploring the dynamics of a simple triangle of great powers, can be of only limited value when applied to the much more intricate constellation of powers which now seems to be taking shape. For a detailed exposition of the various possible patterns of future international conflict, rather more complex models are needed. Those secondary major powers which have been cast for important parts in a global system of more than three powers must be brought into the picture.

7 The Complex Triangle

The idea of a global system of five or six great powers, which many writers and some policy-makers in the West advanced in the early and mid-sixties, gained new currency from several major developments in the international politics of the early seventies. The progress of the Soviet-American Strategic Arms Limitation Talks, which brought the détente between the two rivals of the Cold War to its most advanced stage, the Sino-American rapprochement, which marked an important step in the emergence of China as a third great power, and the increased independence and rising influence of other major powers, particularly Japan and the principal members of the European Economic Community, forced people in most parts of the world to look beyond the still surviving dualistic system and encouraged many to speculate about a system which would be more complex than the great-power triangle discussed in the previous chapter. A number of public pronouncements and spectacular initiatives by the principal decision-makers of the hitherto most influential power in the world gave further incentive to projections of a multiple system. This system was envisaged variously as a pentarchy or hexarchy, as a concert, and as a balance of power. It is still the model of much thinking about the future structure of international politics.

While it is possible to argue that the triangular system has been established already, it would be difficult to maintain that a pentagonal or a hexagonal one actually exists. For the purpose of the present enquiry, the appropriate question must be whether or not it is likely to come about. To answer that, it will be expedient to consider, first, whether the prospective members of such a system are both willing and able to play their parts and, second, whether the various conditions that in the past have proved necessary for establishing and maintaining a system of five or six great powers are present today or likely to arise in the near future.

Judging by a number of public statements, American policy-makers may have been envisaging for some time the emergence of a five-power system, and may even have taken steps to help bring it about. It was late in 1971 that President Nixon made his oft-quoted statement:

> We must remember the only time in the history of the world that we have had any extended period of peace is when there has been balance of power. It is when one nation becomes infinitely more powerful in relation to its potential competitor that the danger of war arises. So I believe in a world in which the United States is powerful. I think it will be a safer world and a better world if we have a strong, healthy United States, Europe, Soviet Union, China, Japan, each balancing the other, not playing one against the other, an even balance.[1]

Subsequently some of Nixon's principal advisers expressed similar views. What is more, the opening of relations with China, the prodding of Japan in the direction of a more independent international role and the encouragement to the countries engaged in the formation of the EEC could be seen as parts of an American effort to realise a scheme of a global structure of five great powers.

However, it does seem likely that the motivation for such pronouncements and initiatives was a desire to preserve the superiority of the United States in the world. If the aim was not so much to set up an 'even balance' as to make up for the loss of strategic superiority by widening the diplomatic options, American policy-makers may have envisaged the role of their country in the projected global balance of power less as an equal among a handful of great powers than as the king-pin of the whole system. They may have imagined a situation in which the United States balanced the Soviet Union and China against each other and at the same time contained both with the help of Europe and Japan. Assuming that the United States possesses the diplomatic skill required for such a part, which even some American writers have doubted, one may wonder whether the strategic strength of the Soviet Union and the political independence of Japan and the principal West European countries may not stand in the way of a successful performance.

At several junctures of the Cold War the Soviet Union found it expedient to call for a concert of more than two major powers to deal with a particular situation of conflict.[2] During the period of détente, too, there have been times when the Russians have seemed to favour the idea of a local concert of a group of major powers, generally to tackle conflict in the Middle East. But in the present situation the Soviet leaders apparently do not wish to encourage any tendencies for the international system to move towards a multiple structure. They have shown no enthusiasm whatever for the American idea of a five-power balance. And their reactions to the Sino-American rapprochement have made it clear that even a triangular system is most unwelcome in Moscow.

That the Soviet government should be reluctant to abandon the dualistic system at this time is understandable. It was just as the Soviet Union was reaching parity of strategic strength with its old opponent of the Cold War that the United States managed to improve its diplomatic position by moving closer to China. If, as seems to be the case, the policy of the Soviet government is to use its strategic parity, or superiority, to maintain its positions in Europe and Central Asia and to increase its influence elsewhere, particularly in the Middle East and the Indian Ocean area and, lately, Africa, then that power can hardly be expected to play a willing part in a system which casts its immediate rival in the role of a third great power and gives the major allies of its traditional rival new and more influential parts to play. Given the emergence of a global triangular relationship and the tendencies towards a more complex system, the Soviet government must be expected to defend the waning dualistic system for some considerable time by concentrating on its dialogue with the American government.[3]

China, of course, ever since the split with the Soviet Union, has been a persistent critic of the dualistic system, which it has seen as leading to both struggle for hegemony and collusion against others. Since its involvement in triangular interaction with the United States and the Soviet Union, it has maintained its verbal opposition to the US–USSR domination of international society, refusing to present itself as a candidate for superpower rank and instead putting itself forward as leader of the middle powers and small states of the world. The obvious political advantages of opposing dual super-power hegemony may well make this the chief line in the foreign policy of China as long as it remains greatly inferior to the two principal powers. But it seems likely that, as China moves a little closer to the Soviet Union and the United States in strategic force and economic power and begins to experience the advantages of being more than a regional power, it will gradually come to claim top rank in the hierarchy of states.

But, even though China eventually may accept in both form and fact a system dominated by three great powers, it is hardly likely to take kindly to the notion of a five-power structure. Though it seems to favour an increase in the political unity and diplomatic influence of the countries of the EEC, it would hardly wish to see an independent and possibly strategically powerful Japan join the group of great powers. While the forces of the West European nations, placed as they are at the rear of China's rival, are likely to help contain the Soviet Union, Japanese power could well present a threat to China. Not only might Japan, China's traditional enemy, become a formidable economic and political rival in various parts of Asia and, if some of its economic and technological power were translated into nuclear capability, even a new threat in military-strategic terms. But also there can be no certainty that this country might not enter into some form of alliance with the Soviet Union, which would present China with the danger of encirclement. So, while the idea of accepting a united Europe into the class of great powers, and thus moving from a triangular to a quadruple system, might have some appeal for the Chinese leaders, the prospect of Japan joining the others in a quintuple system is more likely to inspire their fear.

Since the 'Nixon shocks' in 1971, Japan has found it necessary to reconsider its international position. The emergence of China as a third great power in the global system and the loosening of the former intense relationship with the United States have been strong encouragements for Japanese political leaders to abandon the dualistic conception of world politics and to explore the possibility of taking a more independent part in international relations. The traditional Japanese concern about rank and a growing national self-confidence have acted as further incentives in the search for a new role.

Shortly before his meeting with President Nixon in America early in 1972, Prime Minister Sato, who was in the habit of giving more thought to international politics than his successor, advanced the notion of a balance of five powers as the basis of Japan's future foreign policy. 'Japan, together with America, China, Russia and the European community, make up the concept of a five-power balance seeking to maintain world peace and order', he stated in a press conference. 'As a member of this balance, Japan must play a considerable role.'[4] Some of his ministers, too, paid lip-service to the Nixon-Kissinger doctrine of a multiple balance of power. Subsequently Mr Tanaka echoed his predecessor's statements by declaring his intention of pursuing what he called a 'multipolar diplomacy'. Yet, so far, Japanese leaders have failed to present a clear picture of the role their country might assume in the international system they are projecting. Though there has been a movement away from isolation, the various long-standing reservations about once again becoming involved in Asian power politics do not seem to have been finally overcome. Nor is it at all clear by what means Japan might try to play a new role in the future. While it is becoming increasingly difficult to believe that that country will constantly rely to so large an extent on economic power as a basis for political influence, it is even harder to predict when, how and to what extent it will seriously try to assert itself in military strategic terms as well.

Whatever the degree of determination with which Japanese political leaders have discarded the dualistic view of the world and set out to seek a place for their country in a multiple arrangement, the question remains whether Japan would actually be able to perform a major function in a global system. In addition to the difficulties of formulating a clear foreign policy already referred to, Japan has the handicap of diplomatic inexperience. Its earlier modern tradition of diplomacy, which was developed late in the last century, went into decline after the defeat of Russia and all but expired in the age of militarism. Its more recent tradition, which was initiated during the period of the American occupation, carries the limitation of having been built up almost entirely within the framework of the alliance with the United States. Finally, assuming that Japan could overcome both its political inhibitions and its diplomatic impediment, it would still be up against the problem of finding a way of backing its foreign policies and international conduct with adequate force. The various obstacles and uncertainties that lie in the way of developing a significant nuclear capability would seem to relegate Japan for a long time to a position of considerable inferiority in relation to the three greater powers and to condemn it for many years to a very unequal part in any quintuple system.

The Europe of the EEC, despite a certain degree of success with attempts at economic integration, is still a group of nations rather than a political entity. Its attitudes to developments in the global system have varied from country to country, reflecting the different problems and opportunities of the members of the Community. Yet, the reactions of the principal West European nations to changes in the relations of the great powers have shown some common traits. Both British, West German and French political leaders have at one time or another expressed anxiety about the Russo-American dualism, particularly when it seemed liable to lead to a degree of exclusive cooperation between the superpowers.

British criticism may be said to date back as far as the Teheran Conference of 1943, where Roosevelt's private meetings with Stalin initiated the exclusive relationship of the Big Two. Churchill's account of his reactions to being left out is worth quoting, since it touches on the discord between a dualistic and a multiple conception of international politics:

> The morning of the 29th [November 1943] was occupied by a conference of the British, Soviet, and American military chiefs. As I knew that Stalin and Roosevelt had already had a private conversation, and were of course staying at the same Embassy, I suggested that the President and I might lunch together before the second plenary meeting that afternoon. Roosevelt however, declined, and sent Harriman to me to explain that he did not want Stalin to know that he and I were meeting privately. I was surprised at this, for I thought we all three should treat each other with equal confidence. The President after luncheon had a further interview with Stalin and Molotov, at which many important matters were discussed, including particularly Mr Roosevelt's plan for the government of the post-war world. This should be carried out by the 'Four Policemen', namely, the U.S.S.R., the United States, Great Britain, and China.[5]

In the post-war years, Britain gradually came to accept a secondary place in global politics. The special relationship with the United States, which lasted throughout the Cold War, made it easier for the former great power to tolerate the dualistic system. As the principal lieutenant of one of the Big Two, it had less reason than some of the other European countries to feel excluded. But when eventually the special relationship weakened and Britain moved closer to the Continent, some British political leaders came to share more fully the fear of superpower domination held by many Continental statesmen.

West German leaders, well aware of the possibility that cooperation between the superpowers might give expression to, among other things, a shared concern to limit the arms and restrain the ambitions of Germany, have generally been sensitive to signs of an entente between Russia and America. An early example of this attitude is that of Adenauer, who is said to have been wondering uneasily at the height of the Suez crisis whether the United States was about to enter into agreement with the Soviet Union at the expense of Europe.[6]

But it was in de Gaulle's France that opposition to superpower cooperation took its most determined form. Like Churchill at Teheran, de Gaulle was unwilling to allow the dualistic tendencies to eclipse the older multiple order. In the period of East-West détente, the spectre of a Russo-American 'condominium' haunted his foreign policy almost as much as that of 'collusion' did Chinese policy. His efforts to undermine the dual hegemony and lay the spectre of a superpower conspiracy took various forms. In some situations he found an opportunity to advocate a revival of the post-war concert of the Big Four, as for example in the first stage of the Middle Eastern crisis of 1967.[7] At other times he leaned towards the Soviet Union in an attempt to establish a Europe stretching to the Urals.

The second round of the Strategic Arms Limitation Talks and the preparations for the conferences on security and cooperation in Europe and on mutual and balanced force reductions brought the issue of superpower domination of Western Europe to the fore again. The Nixon-Brezhnev meetings and other sings of a tendency for the governments of the United States and the Soviet Union to negotiate above the heads of their allies strengthened the suspicions of the Europeans and revived their fear of a Russo-American deal. Once again it was the French who showed most concern. But on this occasion, too, the anxiety of the various governments failed to lead to general agreement on the foreign policy to be pursued by the nations of the EEC.

The reasons why Western Europe has been unable to take the part of a powerful and independent unit in the international politics of the world have been partly political and partly strategic. Though the principal powers sometimes have reached a degree of concert on a particular issue, such as that of *Ostpolitik*, where Heath and Pompidou agreed to back Brandt's policy, the conflicting concerns of the members of the EEC have ruled out any such broad and general coordination of policies that would allow the Community regularly to speak with one voice when dealing with the great powers of the world. At present, there are few signs that the various sorts of political disagreement that in the past have stood in the way of diplomatic unity will be overcome.

In military and strategic terms Western Europe has been dependent on the United States since the Second World War. Even now the nuclear weapons of Britain and France have deterrent capacity only to the extent of being enough to 'tear off a limb' in a conflict with the opponent. The keen concern shown by the Europeans at any sign of a development in American foreign policy in the direction of isolationism indicates just how conscious they are that their security against Soviet and East European forces in the last resort depends on the strength and determination of the United States. As with Japan, the need for an American nuclear umbrella seriously restricts the ability of Western Europe to act as an independent power.

To the handicaps of political disunity and strategic dependence must be added economic insecurity. Though well-endowed with other important resources, the EEC is still short of oil. As the energy crisis showed, Western Europe, again in common with Japan, is dependent on the oil-producing countries for the maintenance of its economies. This form of dependence, too, is a serious limitation on international freedom. Indeed, the diplomatic impotence of Western Europe in the war in the Middle East in 1973 called in question its capacity to act as a composite power in other contingencies as well. In global politics, it must be concluded, the Europe of the EEC has neither the political purpose, the strategic capacity nor the economic independence necessary for asserting itself as a principal power.

India, though it may have benefited considerably from the dualistic system, has never been a champion of a world dominated by two superpowers. The Cold War undoubtedly gave India an opportunity to enhance its diplomatic standing by staying out of the conflict and occasionally offering its good offices; but it also exposed that country to much the same dangers as the rest of the world faced. Often Indian leaders of the time were alarmed about the risk of a general conflagration, which they feared might involve non-aligned countries as well. The détente in East-West relations sometimes presented the Indian government with the possibility of increasing its political leverage by playing each superpower against the other; but it also introduced certain prospects which were almost as disturbing to that government as they were to some others. In the sixties many Indians became uneasy about tendencies towards

Russo-American collaboration, which they suspected might turn out to be at the expense of lesser powers, particularly those belonging to the third world.

In recent years, the Sino-Soviet rivalry in the sub-continent has made Indians even more aware than the Japanese of the rise of China and the emergence of a great-power triangle. But India has not yet reached the point of playing the triangular system. Having found it necessary or expedient to lean on the Soviet Union in sub-continental affairs, it has been in no position so far to play China against the Soviet Union. Nor has it been able to take up the even more complicated game which involves also the third of the three great powers – the one de Gaulle, placed on another side of the triangle, attempted in 1963, when he 'played the Chinese card' in order to improve his diplomatic position between the Soviet Union and the United States.[8]

The notion of a global system of five or six great powers does not seem to be an important part of Indian thinking about world politics. Seen from New Delhi, Japan and the principal West European countries figure as middle powers. India itself has a very long way to go before it can be counted a great power. Though the victory over Pakistan and the successful explosion of a nuclear device obviously gave much encouragement to some of the more ambitious circles in Indian political life and no doubt made many of its leaders more aware of India's potential for big-power status, the government still has to concentrate almost exclusively on domestic and sub-continental affairs. Until it has made substantial progress in the solution of its intractable social and economic problems, the Indian government will be unlikely to have either the inclination or the ability to assert itself beyond the region. Even if it developed operational nuclear weapons, India would not become a global power. With its sphere of influence limited to the sub-continent and with its interests extending little beyond this region, the prospect of India assuming a major part in a multiple world balance of power seems even remoter than that of Japan and Western Europe becoming principal actors.

To the extent that the establishment and the operation of the multiple balance of power depend on the existence of five or more great powers which are both willing and able to interact fully at the highest level of international politics, the material for such a system is clearly not available in the world today. We have only two global powers, of roughly equal greatness. One other power, though still essentially a regional actor, has accepted the invitation to play an independent part in a triangular system and has shown some ability for the role. Of these three principal powers, only one, the United States, has projected the multiple system as its goal; and it is very doubtful that the particular conception of a multiple constellation which the government of that country may entertain would be acceptable to any of the other powers, even if they came to think in terms of a multiple system. Below the level of the three principal actors we have a number of important middle powers, one of which, Japan, has declared itself in favour of a global multiple balance of power. Other weaknesses apart, the obvious military and strategic inferiority of these powers and their dependence on the super-powers, with one or the other of which each is involved in an alliance of some sort, make them unable to play an independent part at the global level.

In recent years it has often been asserted that military and strategic strength is less important in international politics than it used to be and that economic power is what really matters in the contemporary world. Thus, it has sometimes been suggested— though more frequently before than after the oil crisis revealed the basis vulnerability of some of the economic giants of the Western world—that Japan and the EEC are so powerful in economic terms that they, despite their various strategic and political handicaps, are fully capable of playing an independent part at the highest level of international politics, and that they, therefore, ought to be regarded as great powers. Certainly, the international relations of the seventies have shown a remarkable shift of emphasis in many parts of the world from matters of national security to economic issues. Yet, the tendency to view rivalry in trade and competition for resources as the essence of global politics and to regard the ability to hold one's own in disputes about currency reform and similar matters as the test of great-powerhood reflects an inclination to overlook the military-strategic framework within which such altercations take place.

Though there were other influences at work, basically it was the emergence of a triangular strategic-diplomatic pattern and the growth of friction on the Sino-Soviet side of the triangle which made it possible to maintain a sufficiently high degree of détente in the various relationships involving the non-Communist powers to allow them to concentrate for the time being on matters of prosperity rather than survival. The United States, enjoying the advantages of having the Communist antagonists compete with each other for its favours, was in a position to develop mutually beneficial economic relations with both parties. The détente between them and the United States gave its principal allies, as well as some of its former satellites, a degree of political independence which they had not enjoyed in the Cold War. Japan and the leading West European nations could now afford not only to challenge the alliance leader in economic matters but also to develop their own relationships with one or both of the former opponents, who were interested in securing a degree of support from these influential third parties as well.

To assume that the current concentration on economic matters is going to be a permanent feature of the international relations of the Western powers is to take for granted that the existing pattern of conflict and distribution of friction in world politics are going to last. The degree of optimism behind the assumption would seem to stem from an over-static view of the great-power triangle. The dynamics of the triangular system could well change the pattern of international conflict in ways which would alter the situation of the non-Communist powers fundamentally. A sharp increase in tension between China and the Soviet Union, for example, would tend to polarise the world, quite possibly to the extent of forcing the other major powers, including even the United States, to take sides. A shift of the centre of friction from the Sino-Soviet side of the triangle to one, or both, of the other sides would also radically change the situations of the non-Communist great and middle powers. Any such transformation of the existing pattern would probably quickly shift the current preoccupation with prosperity and welfare into the background and bring to the fore once again the traditional concern with security and survival—where it was in the Cold War and where it still seems to be in Sino-Soviet relations. If this were to happen, Japan and Western Europe, as well as some other middle powers, would again be likely to appear rather less independent and powerful than they may have done lately.

An international system, however, is not merely the product of the foreign policies and the power resources of its units but also the result of historical circumstances. One could even imagine an extreme case in which the various non-subjective factors that make up a historical situation gave rise to a system which corresponded neither to the inclinations nor to the apparent potentials of most of the powers destined to play principal parts in it. Hence, in order to estimate the likelihood of a multiple system of five or six great powers emerging in the next years, it is necessary to examine also what might be called the objective dimensions of the existing situation, the historical framework within which the powers interact.

Since so many of the advocates of a global multiple system, statesmen as well as writers, seem to have drawn inspiration from the European system of the nineteenth century and, in some cases, actually have held up the old Concert of Europe as their model, it may be useful first to examine the conditions in which that system developed and then to ask to what extent these, or adequate alternative, conditions obtain in the contemporary world.

The particular circumstances which gave rise to the European system of the nineteenth century and shaped its development are well known, having been studied by both historians and political scientists.[9] Firstly, the system rested on a stable territorial balance of power. The equilibrium of Europe, which had been upset by France, had been restored through the defeat of Napoleon and consolidated in the peace treaties. The fact that all of the great powers, even the ex-enemy, broadly accepted the Vienna settlement made it possible for them to agree on a number of adjustments to the territorial order when these became necessary or at least to agree to leave matters pending when, as in the case of the Eastern Question, agreement could not be reached. In this way the system of the balance of power operated fairly successfully for about half a century after 1815.

The second important condition for the establishment and maintenance of the system was the consciousness of shared danger. The statesmen of the Restoration had two great fears, war and revolution. From the history of the French Revolution and the Napoleonic Wars they had learned how closely related those evils were. While revolution might lead to foreign aggression and European war, invasion by foreign armies could prepare the way for revolution. Their fear of European war was largely a fear of French aggression. For half a century after 1815, France was regarded as the potential enemy of Europe, any serious disturbance of its internal tranquillity being treated as an emergency pregnant with dangers for its neighbours in particular and Europe in general. Only after the Franco-Prussian War did it become clear that the threat from France was largely imaginary and that the country which had produced Napoleon was no longer the principal danger to peace.

The fear of revolution, too, turned the eyes of European statesmen towards the country of the Great Revolution. Metternich and Frederick William IV of Prussia, like so many other adherents of the conspiracy theory of revolution, were convinced that Paris was the centre of an international network of subversion. After 1818, when revolutions began to break out in the various parts of Europe that once had been occupied by Napoleon's armies, the Continental governments found that it was not enough constantly to heed the indirect threat from Paris. They also had to deal with the direct pressure which the new forces within each country seemed to put on the entire structure of European society. The revolutionary threat retained its credibility till 1848.

Common fear of war and revolution made for solidarity among the governments. Though most of the time the great powers were engaged in rivalry with each other, they were generally careful to keep tension below the level where disunity might give an aggressor a chance to overthrow the states system or the revolutionaries an opportunity to destroy the social order. After the middle of the century the situation changed. With the memory of general war fading and the threat from France and the danger of revolution proving exaggerated, the motives for restraint gradually disappeared. In some countries, Germany after 1866 being the principal example, the governments eventually joined forces with the nationalist and liberal movements, the governments thus gaining fresh energies and the movements acquiring respectable spearheads. This increase in national unity went hand in hand with an intensification of international rivalry and a decline in European solidarity. Long before the end of the century, the divisions in European politics were again, as they had been before the French Revolution, almost entirely vertical. The bonds that had united the statesmen of the Restoration against international Jacobinism were no longer there.

The fact, too, that the great powers had other outlets for their energy than rivalry and war in Europe played an important part in maintaining the system. One outlet was internal. The industrial revolution, by presenting each country with an opportunity to develop its resources and strengthen its economy, opened up new paths of self-aggrandisement. The quest for economic power, being largely self-absorbing, tended to reduce the craving for territorial expansion in Europe, though not in the world beyond. By drawing energy away from potentially aggressive pursuits on the Continent and reducing the pressure on the frontiers within Europe, it served to curb the tension in the states system and to facilitate a degree of cooperation among the great powers.

The other outlet was external. Hand in hand with industrial progress and economic expansion went colonisation. The great powers situated on the fringes of Europe, especially Britain and Russia but also France, were able to subdue peoples and acquire territories in the world beyond, particularly in Africa and Asia. Though the expansionist pursuits of these powers led them into some rivalry on other continents, their involvement at the periphery of the political world often helped to reduce competition and control tension nearer the centre. Till late in the century, the relative concord in Europe prevailed over the conflict in the world, as at the Berlin Conference of 1884–85, where the powers succeeded in reaching some agreement on African affairs. Eventually, however, rivalry in the world exacerbated tension in Europe. When the power that occupied the central position on the Continent became aware of having been left behind in the race for colonies, it decided to seek a place in the world, even if it meant overturning the balance of power in Europe. The imperialist rivalries of the last decade before 1914 culminated in the First World War.

The influence of a high degree of cultural affinity and some measure of ideological agreement among the powers was of some importance as well. The geographical contiguity and common cultural heritage, the continuous relations and parallel development of the great European nations had produced a fairly homogeneous society. Despite its history of persistent rivalry and frequent wars, nineteenth-century Europe constituted a family of nations. Even the wars, as Dostoievsky and Treitschke pointed out, had been in some ways an integrating force in the international society of Europe. Like family quarrels, they had not only divided the members but also, by teaching them to recognise and respect each other's peculiarities, brought them closer together. The bonds among the nations were sealed by intricate dynastic blood relationships, the results of generations of intermarriage. The supreme manifestation of the cultural and ideological ties and the dynastic links was the Holy Alliance of 1815. Shocked by the French Revolution and overwhelmed by the long wars, all the Christian sovereigns in Europe, except the King of England and the Pope, put their names to the declaration of principles drawn up by Tzar

Alexander. But the Concert of Europe, too, was to some extent the product of a joint outlook. Shared values and some common ideas not only facilitated consultation and cooperation among the sovereigns and ministers of the great powers but also imposed limitations on their altercations and rivalries. Though hardly the most important factors, cultural similarity and ideological compatibility complemented the more substantial forces of cohesion and helped the international system to survive.

Finally, the peculiar composition of the nineteenth-century states system facilitated the successful operation of the balance mechanism. The European system consisted of a group of more or less comparable great powers, who towered over a larger number of small states of varying strength. One of the great powers, Britain, was rather stronger than the others and isolated by water from the rest of Europe. For historical and geographical reasons, this power was not inclined to use its preponderance to subdue the Continent, but content to keep the other powers divided and in check. By playing the part of the balancer, the island power allowed the system to perform its traditional function of upholding, through crises and wars, the independence of the states of Europe and thus to maintain its own *raison d'être*.

The various conditions for the existence of the system were interdependent. Fear of war and concern with economic expansion were closely linked. Similarly, dread of revolution and awareness of a European society based on common values fortified each other. The connection between balance of power in Europe and territorial expansion beyond it is another example. While balance at the centre encouraged expansion on the periphery, the quest for new territories in the world promoted stability and respose in Europe. Such interdependence tended to make the survival of the European system more precarious. A reversal of any one set of circumstances might conceivably undermine the whole structure.

If these were the circumstances that allowed the old European system to come into being and to survive for so long, does the international situation of our time present similar or equally favourable conditions for a multiple balance of power? The first difference worth noting between post-Napoleonic Europe and the contemporary world is that today there is no formally agreed territorial order to provide a basis for such a system. The Second World War did not eventuate in a general peace treaty to which all the principal powers subscribed. Instead it produced a territorial status quo with which no major power was quite satisfied. Thus, the international relations of the post-war decades, much more than those of the Restoration period, have been disturbed by serious territorial disputes as well as by instances of competing intervention in the civil wars of divided nations. True, the two principal powers have remedied the situation to some extent by gradually and tacitly recognising minimum spheres of influence for each other, in the Americas for the United States and in Eastern Europe for the Soviet Union, and by channelling most of their rivalry into regions where such spheres have not been demarcated. But the tentative and informal nature of the agreements they have reached, the geographical narrowness of the spheres of influence they have acquired, and, above all, the fact that, so far, only these two powers possess recognised spheres make such arrangements for controlling conflict a very inadequate territorial foundation for a multiple balance of power. Agreements about spheres of influence, being products of the Cold War, belong to the dualistic system of the superpowers rather than to a multiple system of five or six great powers.

A strong awareness of shared danger, the second condition favouring the post-1815 system, is certainly an important element of the modern situation. But the danger has taken a form rather different from that of the Restoration period. The Second World War did not leave an ex-enemy which for decades could present the former allies with a credible threat to both the international and the social structure of the world. Though the superpowers seem to have recognised a shared interest in preventing the nuclear rearmament of Germany and maintaining the pacification of Japan, neither of them has been able to regard either of the ex-enemies as posing a serious threat to the existing order of the world. China, though it exercises considerable ideological appeal in several diverse quarters and arouses fear in others, still lacks the economic and military power necessary to back an effective programme of world revolution. The Soviet Union, despite its past efforts of subversion and its lingering ideological professions, now has too large a stake in the existing international order to be entirely convincing as a revolutionary power. And the United States, notwithstanding the aggressive style of some of its past policy-makers and the ideological content of various official statements about American foreign policy, is essentially a defensive power. There is no one today to fill the role that the European governments' dread of international

Jacobinism allowed France to play in the age of Metternich.

In the age of nuclear weapons it is above all else the fear of major war which imposes a degree of restraint on the competitive interaction of the principal powers. A general awareness of being exposed to the danger of large-scale destruction, perhaps even obliteration, in an unlimited war with modern weapons has prepared the way for the negotiation of certain formal measures of arms control, particularly the test ban treaties, the non-proliferation treaty and the SALT agreements. As far as the superpowers are concerned, it has also helped to bring about a number of much less formal but possibly rather more important limitations on international conflict. These, as we have seen, may be deduced from the actual conduct and interaction of the Soviet Union and the United States in conditions of international crisis, and may be divided into broad principles of diplomatic strategy and vague guidelines relating to particular situations or special spheres of rivalry.[10] However, it is not to be assumed that such principles and guidelines, which are products of a dualistic relationship and rest at the most on a tacit understanding between the superpowers, will apply equally to a multiple system. Whether they will or not must depend not merely on the willingness of the other members of the prospective system to accept what the superpowers so tentatively have laid down but also on the extent to which these two powers are prepared to adjust their arrangements for conflict to suit the requirements of other great powers.

Are there adequate alternative outlets for the energies of the great powers? For the United States and the Soviet Union, the economic growth race and scientific competition are still encouragements to self-absorption, though less so than in Khrushchev's time, when the Russians were farther behind the Americans and keener to catch up. What may now be more important is that both powers have fairly serious immediate or long-term problems of domestic politics to occupy them. Since Japan until now has chosen to assert itself internationally through economic rather than military-strategic power, its concentration on economic development is not so much an alternative to external ventures as the very basis for its influence abroad. China and India will have to devote the bulk of their energies to economic development and social improvement for many decades. And the countries of Western Europe seem likely to concentrate a good deal of attention for some considerable time on the organisational and other problems tied up with their intention to achieve a higher degree of economic and political integration.

But, though in most cases domestic challenges to the great powers of the future are likely to be both plentiful and demanding, they may not play quite the same role as they did in the nineteenth century. Unlike the old European powers, who were at more or less the same stage of economic development, though with Britain rather more industrially advanced than the rest, the potential members of a new multiple system are as unequal in economic as they are in military-strategic terms. In such a situation, self-involvement would probably make nations even more conscious of belonging to either the rich or the poor countries, more aware of issues stemming from the economic inequality of international society. Though it might drain energy away from some types of aggressive pursuits in the foreign field, such an awareness would be more likely to result in an accentuation of the economic dimension of friction than in a general reduction of international tension. Though, as it has been argued above, there are good reasons to expect that the pattern of economic friction will never eclipse for any length of time the pattern of political tension, any accentuation of the economic dimension would tend at least marginally to reduce friction between the Soviet Union and the United States, both 'have' states, and to increase it between the Soviet Union and China as well as between, for example, Japan and India. The ultimate imaginable effect of a tendency to concentrate on the economic inequalities and social injustices of international society would be a general confrontation between the advanced and the less-developed nations, of which quite a few signs, in the view of some observers, already have appeared in the debates of the United Nations General Assembly and the UNCTAD meetings, as well as in the actions of groups such as OPEC. A sharp division of the world along economic lines, if it were possible, would hardly be conducive to the smooth operation of a multiple balance system, which requires elasticity and mobility. The powers would be too tied by economic considerations to move freely enough to form political anti-hegemonial alliances.

If it is doubtful that the net effect of the internal outlets for energy and ambition will be a reduction in international tension, the difficulty about external outlets is that they are nearly closed in the modern world. In a global system the powers obviously have a much narrower geographical scope for expansion than had the members of the old European system. An intensified competition for economic and political influence in areas outside the accepted spheres of interest is more likely to increase than to reduce tension among the great powers. Exploration and colonisation of space seem far from offering an opportunity of re-establishing the nineteenth-century concord between relative restraint and stability along the internal boundaries between the powers and expansion and rivalry in the less sensitive regions beyond the geographical limits of the states system. The idea of a rivalry in space which will eventually help to reduce tension on earth still belongs to science fiction rather than to practical politics.

Would cultural differences and ideological conflicts interfere with the operation of a global multiple system? Obviously, the international society of the second half of the twentieth century, being universal in principle, does not have the homogeneity of the European society of the nineteenth century. Modern means of transport and communication, a high degree of economic interdependence and the existence of formal international institutions do not make up for the absence of the centuries of shared history and dynastic intermarriage which linked the old European states. A system which comprised the United States and a number of European nations, including the Soviet Union, as well as China, Japan and India could hardly be held together by cultural affinity. Nor could it rest on even that minimum measure of ideological agreement which, despite the differences between the autocracies of the Eastern monarchies and the constitutional systems of the Western powers, helped to hold the old European system together. Whether or not the importance of the ideological element in the conflict between East and West has declined since the Cold War, the communist conception of international order is still difficult to reconcile with that of the West. And in the Sino-Soviet conflict ideology obviously continues to play a major role. Since the multiple system traditionally requires each of its units to be willing and able to change partners fairly freely in response to shifts in the power structure of international society, serious cultural and ideological differences must be impediments to its efficient operation.

The actual composition of the modern states system adds further complications. Firstly, assuming that a balancer is necessary for the successful operation of the multiple balance mechanism, no existing power seems qualified to perform the function nearly so well as Britain did in the European system. Even some American observers have wondered whether the United States, which other writers occasionally have cast for this part, possesses the political detachment and diplomatic skill required.[11] China, though it may have detachment enough, not only lacks the superior power which allowed Britain to balance the old system but also seems insufficiently committed to the idea of a great-power system to be its main prop. Japan occupies a geographical position which in relation to the Asian mainland resembles that of Britain in relation to the European continent, but lacks the necessary power and diplomatic skill. Nor does any other great or major power seem likely to prove a reliable balancer of a multiple system.

Secondly, the marked growth in the number of independent states has radically changed the numerical proportion between great powers and others, with the result that it may now be rather more difficult for the great to manage the small. While in the nineteenth century the lesser powers generally had to accept the decisions of the great, today this does not always seem to be so. Even if the great powers of the future were able to act in concert, the middle powers and the small states of the world would be likely to have more scope for following their own inclinations than was the case with their predecessors in Europe. So, to the extent that the successful operation of the balance-of-power mechanism depends not only on regulating relations among the great powers but also on managing affairs among the lesser ones, conditions for a multiple system now seem less favourable.

However, there is one element of the existing situation which may be even more important than the various shortcomings revealed by an analysis based on comparisons with nineteenth-century Europe. The introduction of nuclear weapons, it can be argued, has largely rendered the complex balance itself obsolete. In the first place, the nature of these weapons has changed the attitude to the use of force. Traditionally, the multiple system worked because each great power in principle was prepared to go to war to defend not only its own but also other states' integrity. Today the principal powers, obviously regarding the avoidance of major war as imperative, seem much more reluctant to resort to open force, especially in cases where neither their own nor their closest allies' vital interests are threatened directly. Secondly, the existing distribution of these weapons has sharply reduced the need for military coalitions. The classical balance-of-power mechanism worked through the formation of alliances to check expansionist powers. Today the central balance, resting on the nuclear parity between the Soviet Union and the United States and on their vast strategic superiority over all other powers, is dualistic and seems likely to remain so for a long time. Since this is a balance of mutual and effective deterrence, it is less dependent on the formation of coalitions. Thus, neither the nature nor the distribution of force in the world of nuclear arms corresponds to the requirements of a multiple balance-of-power system.[12]

Neither the subjective factors nor the objective circumstances of the existing situation, it may be concluded from this analysis, are conducive to the establishment of a global balance of five or six great powers. A multiple system of any of the types that demand relatively high degrees of basic agreement and general cooperation among the chief actors seems a particularly unlikely development. One such system frequently advocated is that of a 'concert of the world', which, according to traditional usage, would mean an informal association of major powers which attempted to manage the international affairs of the world by habitually consulting each other and occasionally coordinating their efforts. Another is that of a 'pentarchy', or 'hexarchy', which presumably would mean a great-power directorate which attempted to discharge functions of a governmental nature in the international society of the world.

In the past, such great-power associations, whether of the looser, managerial or of the more formal, governmental kind, generally originated in major wars. In each of the more recent cases, those of 1815, 1919 and 1945, it was a certain degree of unity among the victorious allies, forged in war-time coalition, together with a common determination to maintain peace, a reaction to the suffering and exhaustion caused by general war, which made it possible for statesmen to respond to the need for a reorganisation of international society by setting up a formal concert of the principal powers. The tasks of controlling the ex-enemies and implementing the peace treaties encouraged the powers to maintain a fairly cooperative relationship in the first post-war years. But as the memory of war faded and the need for solidarity declined, the concert loosened and eventually dissolved. Thus, the post-1945 solidarity of the victorious great powers, which was formalised in the Security Council of the United Nations, broke down in the bloc politics of the Cold War.

Some of the more recent developments, notably the Russo-American détente, the emergence of China as a great power with a seat in the Security Council, and the growing emphasis on economic issues in some key relationships, may not be irreconcilable with the notion of a concert of the world. Yet, it takes a good deal of optimism to detect the coming of such a system. Those observers who see current trends as pointing towards broad and general cooperation among the major states of the world apparently believe that the risk of nuclear war may goad the powers towards solidarity. So far, however, the danger of such a war has not been enough to frighten the powers into a relationship of this nature. If it is at all possible to draw lessons from the pre-nuclear age in this field, the failure of the attempt to revive the Concert of Europe shortly before the outbreak of the First World War suggests that even the definite prospect of a major war is a much weaker impetus to concert than the actual recent experience of such a calamity. In any case, even if—assuming a dramatic turn for the worse in international politics—a series of major crises more dangerous than any experienced so far, or perhaps a limited nuclear war, did prove sufficient to create the unity and determination which in the past have been necessary for bringing great powers close to a state of diplomatic solidarity, the ensuing concert of the world would be unlikely to survive for long if most of the other basic conditions for a multiple system, which have been discussed above, were not fulfilled. Instead of a development towards concert and cooperation among the powers, all we have been witnessing in the seventies may be the shaping of a new pattern of global conflict.

It is also possible to question whether it would be entirely desirable to have a high degree of solidarity of all the major powers of the world. If a general concert, or pentarchy, could be set up, it might well provide a substantial measure of order and perhaps also a long period of peace in international relations. But those results would probably be achieved partly at the cost of curtailing the diplomatic scope of many lesser countries. Certainly, on numerous occasions in the nineteenth century the Concert of Europe performed its functions in the European states system at the expense of smaller states. Though some countries, notably Greece and Belgium, owed their liberty to the joint intervention of great powers, others repeatedly found their endeavours rebuffed and their interests ignored by the European Concert. Often throughout the century the loud self-praise of the great powers was accompanied by indignant, though sometimes suppressed, protests from other states, who complained about selfish behaviour and high-handed attitudes on the part of the powers of the 'Pentarchy' (as those most aware of the inclinations of the great powers to suppress others were in the habit of calling the Concert). Though the partners in a world-wide system of joint control or concerted management probably would find it rather more difficult to override the rights and ignore the interests of middle powers and small states, there is no reason to suppose that they would be any more reluctant to do so than the old European great powers were. In any case, it is difficult to see how they might be able to perform their function of maintaining order in international society efficiently without seriously encroaching upon many other states. Whether or not they used the United Nations as their instrument would probably make little difference in this regard.

Though a general concert of the great powers of the world may be an impossible and, from some points of view, also an undesirable goal, there may still be a place for more limited concerts. One possibility is that of a central concert to deal with a particular set of problems, another that of one or more regional concerts to manage local international issues.

A concert of the former kind has often been advocated as the best way of dealing with the problems arising from the existence of nuclear weapons. But when one, on the one hand, considers the great difficulties with which the Soviet Union and the United States have achieved only very limited progress in the field of arms control and, on the other hand, bears in mind the actual and potential conflicts of interest not only between the two superpowers and the other powers with nuclear weapons but also between all the states already in possession of these weapons and those as yet without them, it is difficult not to be pessimistic about the possibility of setting up an effective nuclear concert. Yet, the idea that the five nuclear powers, perhaps later joined by several members of the steadily growing group of potential nuclear powers, might find some venue for discussing the dangers of nuclear war and their responsibilities in that respect, and that their discussions eventually might lead to some sort of arms control, cannot be dismissed as completely impossible.[13] The serious concern about the risks of unlimited war, which is shared by all the major powers, and the apparent tendency for nuclear powers to come to think in broadly similar terms about the nature and use of their strategic weapons, which has been revealed most clearly in the Russo-American arms control negotiations, may in time produce what one writer has called a 'common strategic ideology'.[14] This, in turn, could conceivably lead to some degree of general agreement on arms control. At best, however, the result of concerted efforts to control the use and prevent the proliferation of nuclear weapons would no doubt be a fairly reluctant and rather mistrustful cooperation. Still, this seems an achievement just possible enough to be worth striving for.

If such a concert for the control of strategic weapons did succeed in moving the danger of nuclear war farther into the background of international relations, the powers would be freer to pursue their rivalries without the constant risk of escalation and disaster. But they would not be able to conduct their relations as if nuclear force had been completely separated from international politics. It would always be as nuclear powers that they interacted. Whatever agreements they might have entered into, in extreme situations one or more of the powers might still decide to resort to the threat, or even the use, of nuclear weapons. Indeed, a concert limited to the control of these weapons might itself be instrumental in bringing about such an eventuality. Since the restraint currently being exercised by the great powers in situations of conflict stems largely from the fear of nuclear war, a concert which seemingly had succeeded in pushing the danger of such a war well into the background might unintentionally reduce the incentive to restraint. The result could be a rise in international tension and a re-appearance of the danger of nuclear war in crisis situations. Thus political conflict could eclipse strategic agreement.

On the other hand, one cannot entirely exclude the possibility that a great-power consensus on arms control in certain circumstances could spill over into the political sphere. For example, it is conceivable that such a consensus, especially if it lasted for some considerable time and led to a series of multilateral agreements, might pave the way for attempts at diplomatic coordination of efforts to manage particular types of international crises. On balance, it seems wiser in present circumstances to seek more concerted arms control than continuously to rely on the danger of nuclear war for making the powers exercise enough restraint to confine their conflict to sub-nuclear levels.

Perhaps rather easier to bring about in the existing situation than a global concert of nuclear powers would be one or more regional concerts to manage local issues. For those major powers whose status in international politics is essentially regional, geographically limited associations might be more suitable than a world-wide arrangement. Also, the dynamics of the emerging triangular system of the principal powers could in certain situations offer scope for the formation of multiple concerts on the sub-systemic level when such an arrangement was not possible in the global system. Those situations would be more likely to arise when tension was unevenly distributed in the great-power triangle. Thus, if two of the three powers engaged each other in intense rivalry, the third might be able to develop a type of relationship with one or both of the rivals which allowed other major powers to join in a local diplomatic concert, if they were so inclined. If, for example, the recent keen tension between the Soviet Union and China lasted and the United States remained in the position of *tertius gaudens*, this power could conceivably form relatively cooperative relationships with one or both of the others. If this happened, certain major powers, finding themselves in an international environment dominated by tendencies towards great-power cooperation, might choose to join the two principal powers in a regional concert, assuming that both of the great powers wanted them to. Some of the strongest countries in Western Europe might in such circumstances form a concert with the Soviet Union and the United States to manage European and perhaps also North African international affairs. If the oil-producing countries failed to maintain their present position of economic domination and Western Europe regained most of the influence it enjoyed before its energy shortage, the Middle East, too, might fall within the scope of such a concert. On the other cooperative side of such a great-power triangle, Japan might concert with China and the United States in the management of South East Asian relations. If the end of war in Indochina has made such an arrangement less impossible, future instability in the region may make it seem more desirable.

Alternatively, if the real centre of tension in world politics turned out to be in Soviet-American relations, it might be China which in the long run would enjoy the advantages of *tertius gaudens* and which might be able to develop relatively friendly relations with one or both of the other great powers. If it maintained a positive relationship with the United States, Japan and other secondary powers in the Pacific region might still be in a position to join the two great powers in a regional concert. If China developed fairly friendly relations with the Soviet Union, other secondary powers, for example India, might be able to enter into concert with them for the purpose of managing Asian affairs.

The creation and survival of such multiple regional concerts would depend very much on the nature of the relationship between the two principal partners. Without some degree of diplomatic coordination between these there would be no basis for a wider concert. But very close cooperation between the two might well preclude a multiple arrangement. If the secondary powers in the vicinity, the potential members of a regional concert, felt restricted and threatened by the partnership of the great, some of them might choose to move closer to the third principal power, the one in the opposite corner of the triangle, rather than to put themselves forward as junior partners in a local association. Secondary powers in such a situation would have problems in common with the other great power. While the former, caught up between the collaborators, would be exposed to the dangers of a local condominium, the latter, in a minority of one among the great powers, would be faced with hostile collusion. All of them would have an interest in separating the two collaborators or, if they could not do that, in trying to organise a diplomatic counter-weight to them. If, in the emerging triangle, the Soviet Union and the United States justified long-standing Chinese accusations by moving closer to each other and entering into understandings above the heads of the principal powers in Europe and the Middle East, some of these powers could be expected to respond favourably to approaches from China and even to make advances of their own. If, on the other hand, the more recent Soviet fears proved justified and the United States and China entered into an entente which was directed against the Soviet Union and which excluded Japan, the latter power might well find it easier to choose between China and the Soviet Union in its Asian policy.

As long as relations between two great powers in a global triangle of this type remain sufficiently cooperative without becoming too close and exclusive, regional concert with local third parties may be within the range of possibilities. But those conditions may not obtain for long. One of the findings of triad theory is that a triangle with one negative and two positive relationships is inherently unstable, and that it is apt to break down because of the inability of the party involved in both of the positive relationships to resist in the long run the pressures from the other parties to commit itself in their conflict.[15] Once this party takes sides, the conflict becomes between two and one. The resulting situation is one in which it is likely to become increasingly difficult for the secondary actors in the system to remain unaligned. They, too, will be under pressure to commit themselves in the central conflict. While some of them may think it in their interest to give their support to the stronger or more aggressive side, others may join the opposite side in an anti-hegemonial alliance.[16] In either case, the outcome will be conventional alliances, of great and lesser powers against other great and lesser powers, rather than diplomatic concerts for regional management. It seems that regional concerts, though probably easier to set up than both a general concert of the great powers and a specialised concert of the nuclear powers of the world, are unlikely to survive for long in the emerging structure of international politics.

The international system that now seems to be emerging on the global scene is a triangle of great powers rather than a pentagon or a hexagon, but a triangle on each side of which one or more middle powers figure prominently. In its most developed form, this system may comprise three major sub-systems, each with its centre in a separate region and each dominated by a different set of principal powers. These regional systems are in different stages of development and present a variety of forms with respect to both number of actors and type of structure. The one that has its centre somewhere in Central or Southern Asia is still polarised, with India leaning towards the Soviet Union rather than balancing between the two communist great-power rivals. The system centring on the European and Middle Eastern region is rather more triangular than it used to be, with the countries of the EEC now enjoying more political independence of the United States and having better relations with the Soviet Union and its East European satellites than in the earlier years of the détente. The system with focus in the East Asian and West Pacific part of the world seems to be rapidly assuming the character of a quadruple balance of power, with Japan adjusting to the new relationship with the United States and developing its economic and political relations with the Soviet Union and China.

The last of these regional systems seems the most important and the most interesting of the three parts of the global triangular system. It is the only one in which all of the principal powers are deeply involved. While China has no major role in Europe and the Middle East and the United States prefers to stay fairly aloof from the rivalry in Central and Southern Asia, the Soviet Union plays a much fuller part in North East and even South East Asia. Hence the West Pacific may be described as the centre of gravity of the global system; and Japan, despite its lack of strategic power, may be said to play a part which is closer to the highest level of power politics than both Europe's and India's.

Though it is interesting to speculate about the future forms of the balances in Europe and Asia, the chief concern must be with the emerging balance of four powers. The present constellation is one in which two of the powers, the Soviet Union and China, oppose each other, while the other two, the United States and Japan, apparently try to balance between the opponents. The attempts of the American and Japanese governments to maintain relatively good relations with both have placed each of these third parties in an unstable triangular relationship with the two rivals. Assuming that the rivalry remains hostile, the United States and Japan, exposed to considerable pressure from both sides, are likely to find it difficult in the long run to maintain an equidistant position between the two communist great powers. Once they give up balancing and choose one side or the other in the Sino-Soviet conflict, the existing triangular balances will collapse. If the two powers were to take the same side, the outcome would be a coalition of three against one. If they were to take opposite sides, the result would be a situation in which two pairs of powers faced each other.

In the former case, a coalition of three of the four powers could be either against the Soviet Union or against China. If the Soviet Union appeared to be in the process of acquiring a definite superiority of strategic weapons and at the same time revealed dangerous expansionist ambitions, the United States and Japan would have a strong encouragement to join China in an anti-hegemonial alliance. To the Japanese, such a division of the powers might be preferable to any alternative, mainly because it would allow them to maintain their security arrangements with the United States without taking them into alliance with their traditional enemy, the Soviet Union, but also because it would strengthen relations with their closest neighbour, China. If, on the other hand, China came to be seen by the others as a rapidly rising nuclear power on the point of presenting a real threat to the order of the world, it might conceivably find itself in a minority of one. But, even in such circumstances, a coalition of the United States, the Soviet Union and Japan would not readily be the outcome. In the first place, such a combination would involve the superpowers in a relationship with each other of a type which cannot easily be reconciled with the record of their past interaction, an analysis of which has been presented above.[17] Secondly, though it would provide a political framework for the efforts of Japan and the Soviet Union to develop mutually beneficial economic bonds, it would be a major departure from the tradition of political conflict between these two countries as well. Thirdly, as a 'rich man's club', such an alliance would undoubtedly provoke much hostility in the Third World, and would therefore have the disadvantage for the allies of tending to strengthen the position of China as leader of the developing countries.

Generally speaking, two against two is the more likely result of a break-down of an unstable quadruple balance.[18] Assuming a continued high level of tension between the Soviet Union and China, the existing quadrangle presents two such possibilities: the United States might join China, and Japan the Soviet Union; or the United States might move closer to the Soviet Union, and Japan to China. Two developments could lead to the first division. If the United States, seeing itself as the balancer of the global system, found it necessary or expedient to support the weaker of the two rivals, it might side with China against the Soviet Union. And if Japan, perhaps as a result of a serious economic challenge from the United States and the EEC and a loss of confidence in the American strategic guarantee, found itself able to suppress its deep aversion for a long-standing enemy, it might conceivably form an entente with the Soviet Union. It is also possible to imagine international developments which might lead to the opposite combinations. On the one hand, if the two strongest powers, despite so many indications to the contrary, discovered a way of overcoming their background of mutual suspicion, they might rise above their recent relationship of restrained conflict in order jointly to meet a Chinese and, possibly, eventually also a Japanese challenge to their shared strategic and political superiority. On the other hand, China and Japan could perhaps in certain circumstances set aside their memories of the past and reduce the political and ideological tensions of the present for the sake of developing a degree of diplomatic cooperation in Asian international politics. In the case of either division of the four powers, one of the suggested developments might itself give rise to the other. Signs of an exclusive concord developing between any two powers would encourage the other two to move closer to each other in order to gain protection against a possible future threat from an unfriendly alliance.

If political rivalry and ideological conflict became less of an obstacle to friendly relations between the two communist great powers than they have been lately and their future leaders managed to establish a new Sino-Soviet alliance, the four powers might again divide into either three against one or two against two. It is just conceivable that the three nuclear have-states would unite against a Japan which was bent on developing strategic nuclear weapons to support a policy of aggression and expansion. Even more unlikely, the three Asian powers might form a coalition to protect their continent against interference from the United States. Here, too, a division of one pair against another seems more likely, in which case the two leading communist powers would face the two principal capitalist states in a new political and ideological conflict of global dimensions.

At any particular time, some of the various logically possible combinations will seem more likely than others. Soon after the rapprochement between Peking and Washington many observers thought that the most probable division was the United States and China against the Soviet Union and Japan. But after the meetings between Brezhnev and Nixon the following year collusion between the two superpowers against the two ascending great powers again seemed to many a distinct possibility. The subsequent shift of prospects and prolongation of suspense could be seen mainly as a result of American efforts to maintain a favourable position in the central triangle by carefully balancing between the two communist rivals. To a lesser extent, they might reflect also a Japanese determination to postpone the difficult decision to choose between the two great powers on the Asian continent. The pattern of alliances that will be the ultimate result of this four-power game of manoeuvering is still a matter for speculation. But once a clear division has come about, it is likely to last for some considerable time. Though there may be much jockeying for position before the schism, for long afterwards a diplomatic revolution may well be an unlikely event.

In existing circumstances, a concert of the four does not seem a probable alternative to the prospect of opposed alliances. As explained above, the dynamics of the central triangle might in certain situations produce regional concerts consisting of two of the three principal powers and one or more major powers. But in the absence of the conditions conducive to the formation of a global concert of great powers, they could hardly bring about an association which comprised all of the principal powers as well as Japan. Any sort of balance which did not involve a grouping of the four powers would be unlikely to last for long. The dynamics of the quadruple system points to an eventual break-down into alliances, more likely of two against two. Once a clear division has been established, other major powers, notably the principal West European countries and India, may find it as hard for long to remain unaligned between the two sides as may the United States and Japan in a sustained conflict between the Soviet Union and China. Thus the emerging global system may be divided ultimately into two opposed alliances.

Neither the post-1815 Pentarchy of the European great powers nor the looser multiple balance of the later years of the Concert of Europe, it may be concluded, is a realistic model for contemporary world politics. Not even the Bismarckian system seems a relevant precedent. This structure, which manifested itself most clearly in the Berlin Congress of 1878, has been described as an attempt by Germany to be both 'master and part of the balance'.[19] If it was an arrangement of this type that President Nixon and Dr Kissinger had in mind when they projected an 'even balance', the decline in the international standing of the United States since the war in Indochina would seem to prevent a realisation of their project by itself. If the paradigm for the future must be found in nineteenth-century European politics, perhaps the post-1894 situation, where the powers divided into opposite alliances, provides the most likely pattern. In that case, the task of contemporary statesmen must be to prevent the world from moving towards a pre-1914 situation.

The analysis of the triangular system and the speculations about future patterns of conflict presented here suggest three lines of pursuit as in need of urgent and sustained efforts. First, optimum stability within both the existing and the emerging structure of international politics must be sought with a view to preventing a general collapse of security and an outbreak of major war. The relationship between equilibrium in the central system and stability in the several sub-systems must be explored. In a complex system of three principal powers and a number of major and minor middle powers, such as the one that now seems to be emerging, this means examining the connection between vertically as well as between horizontally interlocking balances. The former part of the enquiry would take up, for example, the relationship between the central triangle, the regional structure of the Soviet Union, the United States and Western Europe, and the local sub-system of the Middle East. The latter part would deal with, for instance, the three regional structures centring on Europe, Asia, and the West Pacific. In such an investigation, it may be necessary to pay rather more attention to the international roles of secondary and lesser powers than has been customary in the past.

Second, firmer and more comprehensive formal agreements for the control of nuclear weapons must be sought. Eventually also the nuclear powers not taking part in the current SALT meetings as well as the principal potential nuclear powers may have to be brought into arms control negotiations at the highest level. A closer examination of the connection between effective concert on strategic matters and restrained rivalry in the military, political and economic spheres would seem a particularly useful contribution here.

Third, attempts must be made to further clarify those loose principles and informal guidelines for regulating international conflict which seem to have gained a degree of acceptance in the interaction of the superpowers and to extend their application to rivalry which involves also other great powers. To bring implicit rules developed in the dualistic struggle of the fifties and sixties to bear upon the various situations of conflict possible in a future system of three or more great powers may be seen as part of a wider effort to adapt traditional principles of diplomacy to suit a world of a growing number of nuclear powers. All are tasks which demand the attention of political writers as well as statesmen.

Notes

INTRODUCTION

1. Widely used synonyms, or near-synonyms, for 'condominium' are 'coim-perium', 'diarchy', 'duopoly', 'joint hegemony' and 'partnership'. The term 'condominium', and related expressions used in the writings of the sixties, are discussed in 'Condominium and Concert', in Carsten Holbraad (ed.), *Super Powers and World Order* (Canberra: Australian National University Press, 1971) pp. 1–4.
2. 'The Arms Race and World Order', in Morton A. Kaplan (ed.), *The Revolution in World Politics* (New York and London: John Wiley and Sons, Inc., 1962) p. 350.
3. Coral Bell, *The Debatable Alliance. An Essay in Anglo-American Relations* (Chatham House Essays; London, New York and Toronto: Oxford University Press, 1964) pp. 111–13.
4. Arnold Toynbee, 'Thoughts on the Foreign Policy of the United States', *Fact*, vol. iv, issue i (January/February, 1967) p. 6.
5. 'The Arms Race and World Order' (op. cit.) p. 350.
6. *The Debatable Alliance* (op. cit.) p. 111.
7. 'Thoughts on the Foreign Policy of the United States' (op. cit.) p. 9.
8. John Strachey, *On the Prevention of War* (London: Macmillan, 1962) pp. 296–7.
9. Ibid., p. 298.
10. Ibid., p. 299.
11. George Liska, *Imperial America: The International Politics of Primacy*, Studies in International Affairs, no. 2 (Baltimore: The Johns Hopkins Press, 1967) p. 89.
12. Ibid., p. 90.
13. *The Debatable Alliance* (op. cit.) p. 122.
14. 'Condominium and Concert' (op. cit.) pp. 4–10.
15. Khrushchev used such phrases fairly frequently, especially during his last two years in office, after the settlement of the Cuban missile crisis and the opening of the rift with China.
16. Khrushchev's interview with C. L. Sulzberger on 5 September 1961; quoted from *Peking Review*, no. 51 (20 December 1963) p. 16.
17. Khrushchev's exchange with Vice-President Nixon at the opening of the American exhibition in Moscow (*The Times*, 25 July 1959, p. 6).
18. Khruschev's visits to the United States, in particular, gave rise to such denials. Early in 1958, after his return from America, Khrushchev said that it was imperative for an improvement in the relations between the great powers not

to be brought about at the expense of the interests of small states (Nikita S. Khrushchev: *For Victory in Peaceful Competition with Capitalism*, New York: E. P. Dutton & Co., Inc., 1960, p. 65, speech of 22 January 1958). Before setting out for the United States the following year he made the same point in reply to questions from a French and a Belgian journalist (*Let Us Live in Peace and Friendship*. The Visit of N. S. Khrushchov to the USA, September 15–27, 1959, Moscow: Foreign Languages Publishing House, 1960, pp. 23–4, press conference of 5 August 1959). In Washington the next month he roundly asserted, 'We are not pursuing a policy of plotting with the strong against the weaker' (ibid, p. 69), Address to the National Press Club, 16 September 1959).

19. *Public Papers of the Presidents of the United States. John F. Kennedy* (Washington: United States Government Printing Office) 1962, p. 900, television and radio interview, 17 December 1962.

20. See *Public Papers of the Presidents of the United States. Lyndon B. Johnson* (Washington: United States Government Printing Office) 1966, vol. II, p. 1067 (speech of 27 September 1966), for an example of President Johnson's use of the term 'normalization'.

21. President Kennedy once came close to spelling out the shared interest of the superpowers in regard to Germany. In an interview with *Isvestia* in 1961 he told Aleksei Adzhubei, Khrushchev's son-in-law, that the United States would not give nuclear weapons to any country and that he would be extremely reluctant to see West Germany acquire a nuclear capacity of its own. Under pressure from the Russian, Kennedy agreed that in a certain hypothetical, though, he emphasised, unlikely, situation the two superpowers would share a concern about revival of German militarism (*Public Papers of the Presidents*, vol. 1961, p. 751, 25 November 1961).

22. President Nixon found it expedient to make such denials even long before the breakthrough in diplomatic relations with China. See, for example, his statement in a news conference on 4 March 1969 after his return from a visit to Europe: 'Europeans, I found, were greatly concerned by what they called the possibility of a US-Soviet condominium, in which at the highest levels the two superpowers would make decisions affecting their future without consulting them. In fact, one statesman used the term "Yalta." He said, "We don't want another Yalta on the part of the United States and the Soviet Union." Whether his assessment was correct about Yalta or not is immaterial. The point is that Europeans are highly sensitive about the United States and the Soviet Union making decisions that affect their future without their consultation. And that will not happen as a result of this trip.' (*The Department of State Bulletin*, vol. lx, no. 1552, 24 March 1969, p. 238). In later years, after China had been drawn into the global diplomatic game, both President Nixon and Dr Kissinger repeatedly had to insist in public that there was no basis for the charge that the United States and the Soviet Union were jointly establishing a world condominium.

23. *The Super Powers: The United States, Britain and the Soviet Union—Their Responsibility for Peace* (New York: Harcourt Brace, 1944).

24. For examples of opposed conceptions of the superpowers, see Arthur Burns's and Hedley Bull's contributions to *Super Powers and World Order* (op. cit.). Professor Burns opens his discussion of the nature and role of these powers with the statement that, 'A super power is one able to wreck half the world, and

committed upon conditions to do so' (p. xi), and closes by committing himself
to the view of the superpowers 'as sources, however unequally, of *disorder*' (p.
xxi). Professor Bull maintains that the superpowers should be seen not merely
as depositories of a certain degree of armed strength, but as bearers of special
rights and duties, as the 'great responsibles' of international society: 'What the
term super power essentially recognises is the appearance since the end of
World War II of a new class of power, superior to the traditional European
great powers, and alone capable of undertaking the central, managerial role in
international politics they have traditionally played' (pp. 142–3.)

INTRODUCTION TO PART I

1. Oran R. Young, *The Intermediaries. Third Parties in International Crises* (New
   Jersey: Princeton University Press, 1967) p. 10. In his subsequent study of
   bargaining during international crises, Young pointed to a number of
   difficulties about using generic definitions of crisis in empirical analyses of
   international politics and argued the need for identifying crises by other
   criteria as well. Outlining the key characteristics of international crisis from a
   nominalist perspective, he described the phenomenon as 'a process of
   interaction occurring at higher levels of perceived intensity than the ordinary
   flow of events and characterised by: a sharp break from the ordinary flow of
   politics; shortness of duration; a rise in the perceived prospects that violence
   will break out; and significant implications for the stability of some system or
   subsystem (or pattern of relationship) in international politics' (Oran R.
   Young, *The Politics of Force. Bargaining During International Crises*, New Jersey:
   Princeton University Press, 1968, p. 15).
2. Coral Bell, *The Conventions of Crisis. A Study in Diplomatic Management* (The
   Royal Institute of International Affairs; London, Oxford, New York: Oxford
   University Press, 1971) p. 9. In Thomas Schelling's view, the essence of crisis is
   its unpredictability: 'It is the essence of a crisis that the participants are not
   fully in control of events; they take steps and make decisions that raise or lower
   the danger, but in a realm of risk and uncertainty'. (Thomas C. Schelling,
   Arms and Influence, New Haven and London: Yale University Press, 1966,
   p. 97).
3. For classification of crises along these lines, see Young, *The Intermediaries* (op.
   cit.) pp. 22–5.
4. *The Conventions of Crisis* (op. cit.) p. 7.

CHAPTER 1

1. Merry and Serge Bromberger, *Secrets of Suez*, trans. James Cameron (London:
   Sidgwick & Jackson Ltd., 1957) p. 147.
2. Herman Finer, *Dulles over Suez. The Theory and Practice of his Diplomacy* (London:
   Heinemann, 1964) p. 434. Finer thought this an excellent summary of the
   American policy.

3. *Secrets of Suez* (op. cit.) p. 159.
4. *Dulles over Suez* (op. cit.) p. 410.
5. Ibid., p. xi.
6. *Dulles over Suez* (op. cit.) p. 368.
7. *Documents on International Affairs, 1956*, ed. Noble Frankland, (Royal Institute of International Affairs; London, New York, Toronto: Oxford University Press, 1959) p. 287.
8. Ibid., pp. 292–4.
9. Ibid., pp. 280–1.
10. Ibid., pp. 288–9.
11. *United States Policy in the Middle East, September 1956–June 1957. Documents*, Department of State Publications 6505, Near and Middle Eastern Series 25, released August 1957, pp. 215–16.
12. Hans Speier, 'Soviet Atomic Blackmail and the North Atlantic Alliance', *World Politics*, vol. ix, no. 3 (April 1957) pp. 318–21 and 326–7.
13. Walter Z. Laqueur, *The Soviet Union and the Middle East* (London: Routledge and Kegan Paul, 1959) pp. 239–40. On Soviet timing, see also Speier, 'Soviet Atomic Blackmail and the North Atlantic Alliance' (op. cit.) p. 324, and O. M. Smolansky, 'Moscow and the Suez Crisis, 1956: A Reappraisal', *Political Science Quarterly*, vol. lxxx, no. 4 (December 1965) pp. 591–3.
14. *Secrets of Suez* (op. cit.) p. 150.
15. *The Memoirs of the Rt. Hon. Sir Anthony Eden. Full Circle*, (London: Cassell, 1960) p. 555.
16. 'Moscow and the Suez Crisis, 1956: A Reappraisal' (op. cit.) p. 596.
17. Ibid., pp. 596–7.
18. M. S. Venkataramani, 'Oil and US Foreign Policy During the Suez Crisis 1956–7', *International Studies*, vol. ii, no. 2 (New Delhi, October 1960) p. 139, note. The author refers to Eugene Rabinowitch's article, 'The First Year of Deterrence' in *Bulletin of the Atomic Scientists*, no. 13 (January 1957) pp. 2–8.
19. 'Moscow and the Suez Crisis, 1956: A Reappraisal' (op. cit.) p. 598.
20. *Dulles over Suez* (op. cit.) pp. 417–18 and 430–1.
21. Hugh Thomas, *The Suez Affair* (London: Weidenfeld & Nicolson, 1966–67) p. 142.
22. Robert Murphy, *Diplomat Among Warriors* (Garden City: Doubleday & Co., 1964) pp. 390–1. On the effect of Bulganin's threats upon the American administration, see the detailed account by Charles J. V. Murphy, 'Washington and the World', *Fortune*, vol. lv, no. 1 (January 1957) pp. 78ff.
23. *Documents on International Affairs, 1956* (op. cit.) pp. 294–5.
24. On Eisenhower's response to the Soviet threat, see 'Moscow and the Suez Crisis, 1956: A Reappraisal' (op. cit.) p. 599; Paul Johnson, *The Suez War* (London: Macgibbon & Kee, 1957) p. 124; *Secrets of Suez* (op. cit.) p. 152; and *Dulles over Suez* (op. cit.) pp. 420–1.
25. *Dulles over Suez* (op. cit.) pp. 432–3.
26. G. Barraclough, *Survey of International Affairs, 1956–58* (Royal Institute of International Affairs; London, New York, Toronto: Oxford University Press, 1962) p. 61.
27. *Documents on International Affairs, 1956* (op. cit.) pp. 270–1.
28. J.-R. Tournoux, *Secrets d'Etat* (Paris: Librairie Plon, 1960) p. 165, and *Secrets of Suez* (op. cit.) p. 152.

29. *The Suez War* (op. cit.) p. 125, and *Secrets of Suez* (op. cit.) p. 153.
30. *Secrets d'Etat* (op. cit.) p. 168. The extract of conversation quoted is a paraphrase.
31. *The Suez Affair* (op. cit.) p. 143, and *Dulles over Suez* (op. cit.) p. 432.
32. *Dulles over Suez* (op. cit.) p. 422.
33. For details of the American financial pressure on the British government, see the memoirs of Harold Macmillan, the Chancellor of the Exchequer. Macmillan thinks that the Federal Reserve Bank played an important part in maintaining the run on the pound and describes Washington's obstruction of Britain's application for an urgent loan from the International Monetary Fund as 'altogether unworthy' (*Riding the Storm, 1956–1959*, London, Melbourne and Toronto: Macmillan, 1971, p. 164). Yet he does not admit that such pressure was decisive in making the British government agree to a cease-fire (ibid., pp. 165–6).
34. On American oil strategy and relations with Britain and France during the crisis, see 'Oil and US Foreign Policy During the Suez Crisis 1956–57 (op. cit.) pp. 132–9.
35. *Full Circle* (op. cit.) p. 561.
36. *Secrets d'Etat* (op. cit.) p. 169. Finer follows Tournoux in his account of this conversation (*Dulles over Suez*, op. cit., p. 429).
37. *Documents on International Affairs, 1956* (op. cit.) p. 268.
38. *The Politics of Force* (op. cit.) p. 55. Oran Young excludes the Suez crisis from his study on the grounds that it was essentially a case of superpower coordination rather than opposition.

CHAPTER 2

1. John R. Thomas, 'Soviet Behavior in the Quemoy Crisis of 1958', *Orbis*, vol. vi (spring 1962) no. 1, p. 61.
2. Donald S. Zagoria, *The Sino-Soviet Conflict 1956–1961* (Princeton University Press, 1962) pp. 201–17.
3. Alice Langley Hsieh, *Communist China's Strategy in the Nuclear Age* (Englewood Cliffs, N. J.: Prentice-Hall, Inc., Rand Corporation, 1962) p. 122.
4. Harold C. Hinton, *Communist China in World Politics* (London, Melbourne: Macmillan, 1966) pp. 38–40 and 266–8. See also a more recent work, J. H. Kalicki, *The Pattern of Sino-American Crises. Political-Military Interactions in the 1950s* (Cambridge University Press, 1975), where the author finds that Moscow successfully applied political-military pressure on Peking to prevent it from forcing the American hand in 1958.
5. Morton H. Halperin and Tang Tsou, 'The 1958 Quemoy Crisis', in Morton H. Halperin (ed.) *Sino-Soviet Relations and Arms Control* (Cambridge, Mass.: M.I.T. Press, 1967) pp. 265–303; see also Morton H. Halperin, *China and the Bomb* (London: Pall Mall Press, 1965) pp. 55–62 (on the Sino-Soviet debate of 1963 on the 1958 crisis).
6. *Survey of International Affairs* (op. cit.) p. 567.
7. Ibid., p. 567.
8. *Documents on International Affairs, 1958*, ed. Gillian King (Royal Institute of

International Affairs; London, New York, Toronto: Oxford University Press, 1962) p. 178.

9. *Survey of International Affairs* (op. cit.) p. 568.

10. *Documents on International Affairs, 1958* (op. cit.) p. 193.

11. Tang Tsou, 'The Quemoy Imbroglio: Chiang Kai-shek and the United States', *The Western Political Quarterly*, vol. xii, no. 4 (December 1959) pp. 1083 and 1085; also, *The Politics of Force* (op. cit.) p. 102, in which Young states that the physical restraints included American efforts to restrict, for example, the supply of jet fuel to the Nationalists, but says that ultimately the political restraints were the more important.

12. *Documents on International Affairs, 1958* (op. cit.) pp. 209–10.

13. A. Doak Barnett, *Communist China and Asia. Challenge to American Policy* (publ. for the Council on Foreign Relations, Harper & Brothers; London: Oxford University Press, 1960) p. 412.

14. Ibid., p. 413.

15. *Survey of International Affairs* (op. cit.) p. 573.

16. *The Politics of Force* (op. cit.) p. 290.

17. *Documents on International Affairs, 1958* (op. cit.) pp. 207–8.

18. *Communist China and Asia* (op. cit.) p. 412.

19. *Documents on International Affairs, 1958* (op. cit.) p. 372.

20. Ibid., pp. 179–82.

21. *Survey of International Affairs* (op. cit.) p. 569.

22. *Documents on International Affairs, 1958* (op. cit.) pp. 215–16.

23. Ibid., pp. 182–9.

24. See above, p. 42.

25. *Documents on International Affairs, 1958* (op. cit.) pp. 195–7.

26. Ibid., pp. 197–204.

27. Ibid., p. 197, note.

28. *The Situation in the Taiwan Area. Position of the Soviet Union.* Soviet Booklet no. 41 (October 1958) pp. 15–16.

29. *The Politics of Force* (op. cit.) p. 154.

30. 'Soviet Behavior in the Quemoy Crisis of 1958' (op. cit.) p. 52.

CHAPTER 3

1. For views on the Soviet motives, see, e.g., Zbigniew Brzezinski, 'Cuba in Soviet Strategy', *The New Republic* (3 November 1962) p. 7; Arnold L. Horelick, 'The Cuban Missile Crisis. An Analysis of Soviet Calculations and Behavior', *World Politics*, vol. xvi, no. 3 (April 1964) pp. 364–77; and Morton Schwartz, 'The Cuban Missile Venture', in James B. Christoph and Bernard E. Brown (eds.), *Cases in Comparative Politics*, 2nd ed. (Boston: Little, Brown & Co., 1969) pp. 268–301.

2. *Documents on International Affairs, 1962*, ed. D. C. Watt (Royal Institute of International Affairs; London, New York, Toronto: Oxford University Press, 1971) pp. 211–12.

3. Ibid., pp. 217–18.

4. Ibid., pp. 221–2.

5. Ibid., pp. 222–3.
6. Ibid., pp. 225–6.
7. Ibid., p. 223.
8. Ibid., pp. 207–11.
9. Ibid., pp. 215–17.
10. Roger Hilsman, 'The Cuban Crisis: How Close We Were to War', *Look*, vol. 28, no. 17 (25 August 1964) p. 20.
11. Henry M. Pachter, *Collision Course: The Cuban Missile Crisis and Coexistence* (London: Pall Mall Press, 1963) p. 209.
12. *The Politics of Force* (op. cit.) p. 208.
13. *Collision Course* (op. cit.) p. 209.
14. *Documents on International Affairs, 1962* (op. cit.) p. 226.
15. In the seven days from 22 till 28 October ten messages were despatched, five each way; but only the last four were published at the time. Robert Kennedy quoted or paraphrased crucial passages of the secret correspondence in his memoir of the crisis; and in 1973 the State Department published all the letters.
16. *Department of State Bulletin*, 19 November 1973, p. 635.
17. Ibid., p. 637.
18. Ibid., p. 638. (The quotations are from the informal translation, which was made immediately available to President Kennedy.)
19. Ibid., p. 639.
20. Ibid., pp. 640–2 (informal translation).
21. *Documents on International Affairs, 1962* (op. cit.) pp. 227–9.
22. *Collision Course* (op. cit.) pp. 50–1.
23. Andrés Suárez, *Cuba: Castroism and Communism, 1959–1966* (Cambridge, Mass., and London: M.I.T. Press, 1967) p. 171.
24. Adlai Stevenson had suggested in a meeting of the 'Ex-Comm' on 20 October that the United States might offer to withdraw its Turkish and Italian Jupiter missile bases in return for a Soviet withdrawal of the Cuban missile bases (Graham T. Allison, *Conceptual Models and the Cuban Missile Crisis: Rational Policy, Organization Process, and Bureaucratic Politics*, Rand Corporation Paper No. P-3919, August 1968, pp. 54–5; see also Theodore Sorensen, *Kennedy*, New York: Harper and Row, 1965, pp. 695–6). Walter Lippmann had mooted the same idea as late as 25 October (D. C. Watt, *Survey of International Affairs, 1962*, Royal Institute of International Affairs; London, New York, Toronto: Oxford University Press, 1970, p. 65).
25. *Documents on International Affairs, 1962* (op. cit.) pp. 226–7.
26. Ibid., pp. 229–30.
27. Ibid., pp. 230–4.
28. Ibid., pp. 234–5.
29. Ibid., p. 235.
30. Robert Francis Kennedy, *Thirteen Days: A Memoir of the Cuban Missile Crisis* (New York: W.W. Norton, 1969) p. 126.
31. When some Russian freighters in the Atlantic slowed down on 24 October, the American government refrained from trumpeting the Russian hesitation to the press (*Collision Course*, op. cit. p. 43). After the relief set in in Washington on 28 October, Dean Rusk briefed reporters off the record: 'If there is a debate, a rivalry, a contest going on in the Kremlin over how to play this situation, we

don't want the word "capitulation" used, or any gloating in Washington to strengthen the hands of those in Moscow who wanted to play this another way.' (Elie Abel, *The Missiles of October: The Story of the Cuban Missile Crisis 1962*, London: Mayflower-Dell, 1966, p. 181). And even after it was all over, President Kennedy 'permitted no crowing that would cause the Soviet to eat crow'. (This phrase appeared in the final paragraph of an early published version of Robert Kennedy's *Thirteen Days*; see the American Magazine *McCall's*, vol. cvi, no. 2 (November 1968) p. 173.)

32. *Documents on International Affairs, 1962* (op. cit.) pp. 235–6.
33. *Cuba: Castroism and Communism* (op. cit.) p. 172.
34. *Documents on International Affairs, 1962* (op. cit.) p. 244.
35. *The Missiles of October* (op. cit.) p. 187.
36. *Documents on International Affairs, 1962* (op. cit.) p. 288.
37. This may have been Mr McNamara's idea when he, in the aftermath of the Cuban missile crisis, remarked that 'there is no longer any such thing as strategy, only crisis management'. (Coral Bell, *The Conventions of Crisis: A Study in Diplomatic Management*, The Royal Institute of International Affairs; London, Oxford, New York: Oxford University Press, 1971, p. 2.).

CHAPTER 4

1. *UN Monthly Chronicle*, United Nations Office of Public Information, vol. iv. no. 6 (June 1967) p. 12.
2. *The Times* (London), 25 May 1967, p. 8.
3. Patrick Gordon Walker has revealed that some prominent members of the British Cabinet at one stage entertained the idea of Britain attempting to break the blockade on its own (*The Cabinet*, London: Fontana/Collins, 1972, p. 138).
4. Nadav Safran, *From War to War. The Arab-Israeli Confrontation, 1948–1967* (New York: Western Publishing Company, Inc. (Pegasus), 1969) pp. 275–8. Safran gives a plausible account of the part the Soviet Union may have played in the initiation of the crisis.
5. Ibid., p. 269.
6. Ibid., pp. 294–5.
7. Walter Laqueur, *The Road to War, 1967* (London: Weidenfeld & Nicolson, 1968) pp. 178–9.
8. Lyndon Baines Johnson, *The Vantage Point. Perspective of the Presidency 1963–1969* (New York: Holt, Rinehart & Winston, 1971) p. 291.
9. Randolph and Winston Churchill, *The Six Day War* (London: Heinemann, 1967) p. 47.
10. *The Vantage Point* (op. cit.) p. 294.
11. Ibid., p. 290.
12. *New York Times*, 24 May 1967, pp. 1 and 16; see also *From War to War* (op. cit.) p. 269.
13. *The Vantage Point* (op. cit.) p. 293.
14. *From War to War* (op. cit.) p. 314.
15. *The Vantage Point* (op. cit.) p. 291.
16. *From War to War* (op. cit.) pp. 301 and 314.

17. *The Road to War, 1967* (op. cit.) pp. 171, 181 and 234; Oran R. Young, 'Intermediaries and Interventionists: Third Parties in the Middle East Crisis', *International Journal*, C.I.I.A., vol. xxiii, no. 1 (winter 1967–68) pp. 53 and 56.
18. *UN Monthly Chronicle*, vol. iv, no. 7 (July 1967) p. 32.
19. *The Vantage Point* (op. cit.) p. 298.
20. Ibid., p. 301.
21. Ibid., p. 302.
22. Ibid., pp. 302–3.
23. Ibid., p. 298.
24. *The Six Day War* (op. cit.) p. 148.
25. Ibid., p. 148.
26. Ibid., pp. 158–9.
27. *The Vantage Point* (op. cit.) p. 301.
28. 'Intermediaries and Interventionists' (op. cit.) pp. 59–60.
29. *The Vantage Point* (op. cit.) p. 300.
30. The Churchills state that a dozen messages were exchanged over the hot line during the course of the week (*The Six Day War*, op. cit., p. 148).
31. *From War to War* (op. cit.) pp. 411–17. Safran's summary of the Podgorny-Nasser talks is based on Eric Rouleau's account in *Le Monde*, Sélection hebdomadaire, 1–7 February 1968.
32. *From War to War* (op. cit.) p. 412.
33. *New York Times*, 20 June 1967, p. 19c.
34. *From War to War* (op. cit.) p. 412. Kosygin made the statement in an interview with the editor of *Life* magazine (2 February 1968, p. 30).
35. *The Vantage Point* (op. cit.) p. 484.

CHAPTER 5

1. See, e.g., Alastair Buchan, 'Crisis Management: The New Diplomacy' (1966), *The Atlantic Papers* (University Press of Cambridge, Mass., 1970) pp. 293–356. The author explains that it was the avowed American intention of retaining as much freedom of action as possible in a crisis which had provided the impetus 'to consider ways in which her allies can share not only in discussion of different actions that might be taken in different contingencies before a crisis occurs but in the handling of the decisions about responses when the crisis has started' (p. 300). Collective management by the NATO allies of East-West crises was his main concern.
2. For an example of the notion of unequal condominium, see *Imperial America: The International Politics of Primacy* (op. cit.).
3. *The Conventions of Crisis* (op. cit.) Ch. 5.
4. See especially *The Politics of Force: Bargaining During International Crises* (op. cit.). Oran Young excludes the Suez crisis from his study on the grounds that it was essentially a case of superpower coordination rather than opposition (see p. 55).
5. See James A. Robinson, 'Crisis Decision-Making: An Inventory and Appraisal of Concepts, Theories, Hypotheses, and Techniques of Analysis', *Political Science Annual*, no. 2 (1969) pp. 111–48. In this review article, the author discusses some of the problems and difficulties of studying international crises.

CHAPTER 6

1. The attitudes of the three powers to the various forms of the multiple system will be discussed in more detail below, pp. 131–4.
2. 'Condominium and Concert', in *Super Powers and World Order* (op. cit.)
3. Martin Wight, *Systems of States*, ed. Hedley Bull (Leicester University Press, 1977) p. 179.
4. See above, pp. 4–6.
5. See below, pp. 141–51 where the section of 'Condominium and Concert' that deals with the conditions for great-power concert (*Super Powers and World Order*, op. cit., pp. 10–22) is reproduced in a somewhat expanded form.
6. 'Peace Kept by Terror: The Superpowers' Moscow Agreements on Strategic Nuclear Forces' (unpublished paper).
7. This term was used by Georg Simmel, the pioneer of triad theory (see Theodore Caplow, *Two Against One: Coalitions in Triads*, Englewood Cliffs, N. J.: Prentice-Hall Inc., 1968, especially Ch. ii).
8. *The Conventions of Crisis* (op. cit.) p. 64.

CHAPTER 7

1. *Time*, 3 January 1972, p. 9.
2. See, e.g., Bulganin's message to Eisenhower of 17 November 1956 (*Suez and the Middle East*, Documents, a Second Collection, covering November 5 to December 9, 1956, Soviet News Booklet no. 25, pp. 21–2), the note to the American Embassy in Moscow from the Soviet Ministry of Foreign Affairs of 11 February 1957 (*United States Policy in the Middle East. September 1956—June 1957, Documents*, Department of State Publications no. 6505, Near and Middle Eastern Series 25, released August 1957, p. 76), and Khrushchev's message to Eisenhower of 7 September 1958 (*Documents on International Affairs*, 1958, (op. cit.) pp. 182–9).
3. Ian Clark has suggested that the Soviet government may be willing to comply with a modified triangular system as long as the American government recognises the special status of US-USSR dialogues on certain mainstream issues ('Sino-American Relations in Soviet Perspective', *Orbis*, vol. xvii, summer 1973, no. 2, pp. 490–2).
4. *The Australian*, 4 January 1972, p. 1.
5. *The Second World War*, vol. v (London: Cassell & Co., 1952) p. 320.
6. See above, p. 20.
7. See above, pp. 77–8.
8. For details of de Gaulle's move in this game, see W.A.C. Adie, ' "One World" Restored? Sino-American Relations on a New Footing', *Asian Survey*, vol. xii, no. 5 (May 1972) pp. 373–4.
9. See, e.g., F. H. Hinsley, *Power and the Pursuit of Peace: Theory and Practice in the History of Relations between States* (Cambridge University Press, 1963); George Liska, *Europe Ascendant: The International Politics of Unification* (Baltimore: The Johns Hopkins Press, 1964); Stanley Hoffmann, *Organisations internationales et pouvoirs politiques des Etats* (Cahiers de la Fondation Nationale des Sciences

Notes

Notes

Notes

Notes 173

Politiques, no. 52, Paris, Armand Colin, 1954); and R. N. Rosecrance, *Action and Reaction in World Politics: International Systems in Perspective* (Boston: Little, Brown & Co., 1963).

10. See above, Ch. 5.
11. See, e.g.. *Imperial America: The International Politics of Primacy* (op. cit.) pp. 88–90, and Stanley Hoffmann, 'Will the Balance Balance at Home?', *Foreign Policy*, no. 7 (Summer 1972) pp. 60–86.
12. For a fuller explanation of these points, see Stanley Hoffmann: 'Weighing the Balance of Power', *Foreign Affairs*, vol. 50, no. 4 (July 1972) pp. 621–6.
13. See, e.g., Hedley Bull's proposal for a conference of the five nuclear powers (*The Moscow Agreements and Strategic Arms Limitation*, Canberra Papers on Strategy and Defence, no. 15, Canberra: Australian National University Press, 1973, p. 29).
14. Coral Bell, 'The Adverse Partnership', *Super Powers and World Order* (op. cit.) pp. 29–31.
15. See, e.g., *Two Against One: Coalitions in Triads* (op. cit.) p. 79.
16. The typical roles open to secondary powers in various situations of the triangular system are outlined in my 'Middle-Power Roles in Great-Power Triangles', *The Year Book of World Affairs 1976* (London) vol. 30, pp. 116–32.
17. See Part One, especially Ch. 5.
18. For a brief explanation why a four-states system tends to set into two pairs, see P.A. Reynolds, *An Introduction to International Relations* (London: Longman, 1971) p. 206.
19. Hoffmann, 'Weighing the Balance of Power' (op. cit.) p. 642.

Index